Data Science Solutions on Azure

Tools and Techniques Using Databricks and MLOps

Julian Soh
Priyanshi Singh

Apress®

Data Science Solutions on Azure: Tools and Techniques Using Databricks and MLOps

Julian Soh
Olympia, WA, USA

Priyanshi Singh
New Jersey, NJ, USA

ISBN-13 (pbk): 978-1-4842-6404-1
https://doi.org/10.1007/978-1-4842-6405-8

ISBN-13 (electronic): 978-1-4842-6405-8

Managing Director, Apress Media LLC: Welmoed Spahr
Acquisitions Editor: Smriti Srivastava
Development Editor: James Markham
Coordinating Editor: Shrikant Vishwakarma

Cover designed by eStudioCalamar

Cover image designed by Pexels

Distributed to the book trade worldwide by Springer Science+Business Media LLC,
1 New York Plaza, Suite 4600, New York, NY 10004. Phone 1-800-SPRINGER, fax (201) 348-4505, e-mail orders-ny@springer-sbm.com, or visit www.springeronline.com. Apress Media, LLC is a California LLC and the sole member (owner) is Springer Science + Business Media Finance Inc (SSBM Finance Inc). SSBM Finance Inc is a **Delaware** corporation.

For information on translations, please e-mail booktranslations@springernature.com; for reprint, paperback, or audio rights, please e-mail bookpermissions@springernature.com.

Apress titles may be purchased in bulk for academic, corporate, or promotional use. eBook versions and licenses are also available for most titles. For more information, reference our Print and eBook Bulk Sales web page at http://www.apress.com/bulk-sales.

Any source code or other supplementary material referenced by the author in this book is available to readers on GitHub via the book's product page, located at www.apress.com/978-1-4842-6404-1. For more detailed information, please visit http://www.apress.com/source-code.

Printed on acid-free paper

Thank you to my parents, Sudha Singh and Omveer Singh, for their undying love and limitless sacrifices to give me the best opportunities in life and helping me live my dreams. Thank you to Daniel Fay, my fiancé, for always empowering me and helping me become the best version of myself. Special thanks to my friend/coauthor/mentor Julian Soh, who inspired me to write my first book and provided great guidance and insights. It's a beautiful journey to see yourself becoming an author, and I would like to dedicate this book to those who stay curious and hungry for knowledge.

—Priyanshi

Thank you to my family – Priscilla, Jasmine, and Makayla – for their continued support and all the great people I have had the honor to learn from, especially my coauthor and colleague, Priya. I also dedicate this book to those using technology to make the world a better place.

—Julian

Table of Contents

About the Authors

Julian Soh is a Cloud Solutions Architect with Microsoft, focusing in the areas of artificial intelligence, cognitive services, and advanced analytics. Prior to his current role, Julian worked extensively in major public cloud initiatives, such as SaaS (Microsoft Office 365), IaaS/PaaS (Microsoft Azure), and hybrid private-public cloud implementations.

Priyanshi Singh is a data scientist by training and a data enthusiast by nature, specializing in machine learning techniques applied to predictive analytics, computer vision, and natural language processing. She holds a master's degree in Data Science from New York University and is currently a Cloud Solutions Architect at Microsoft helping the public sector to transform citizen services with artificial intelligence. She also leads a meetup community based out of New York to help educate public sector employees via hands-on labs and discussions. Apart from her passion for learning new technologies and innovating with AI, she is a sports enthusiast, a great badminton player, and enjoys playing billiards. Find her on LinkedIn at `www.linkedin.com/in/priyanshi-singh5/`.

About the Technical Reviewers

 **David Gollob** has over 35 years of experience working in database and analytics systems. After receiving his degree in Math and Computer Science at the University of Denver, Dave worked as a principal consultant for numerous Fortune 100 companies, helping them to develop enterprise business solutions, highly scalable OLTP systems, and data warehouse and analytics systems. Dave's vendor tour started with Sybase, where he participated in two patents for his work at TCI Corporation focused on billing and distributed systems design. At Sybase, Dave also spent 1.5 years in Switzerland as the Principal Architect. In 1996, Dave joined Microsoft, where he remains today. Dave's work at Microsoft includes both his delivery as a Principal Consultant as well as Managing Consultant where he founded the Microsoft Telecom Practice. Dave has presented and participated in numerous industry events, panel discussions, Microsoft technical events, and product review and feedback cycles. Today, Dave travels the western states visiting state and local government customers, assisting with data, advanced analytics, and AI architecture planning and solutions design. Dave enjoys his time with his family as well as mountain biking, skiing, hiking, and fishing in Colorado.

Bhadresh Shiyal is an Azure Data Architect and Azure Data Engineer and, for the past 7+ years, he is working with a big IT MNC as a Solutions Architect. He has 18+ years of IT experience, out of which for 2 years he worked on an international assignment from London. He has rich experience in application design, development, and deployment. He has worked on various technologies, which include Visual Basic, SQL Server, SharePoint technologies, .NET MVC, O365, Azure Data Factory, Azure Databricks , Azure Synapse Analytics, Azure Data Lake Storage Gen1/Gen2, Azure SQL Data Warehouse, Power BI, Spark SQL, Scala, Delta Lake, Azure Machine Learning, Azure Information Protection, Azure .NET SDK, Azure DevOps, and so on.

He holds multiple Azure certifications that include Microsoft Certified Azure Solutions Architect Expert, Microsoft Certified Azure Data Engineer Associate, Microsoft Certified Azure Data Scientist Associate, and Microsoft Certified Azure Data Analyst Associate.

CHAPTER 1

Data Science in the Modern Enterprise

Data science is the hottest trend in IT, and it is not showing signs of cooling down anytime soon. It is often used as a catchall phrase for all latest innovation, such as machine learning (ML), artificial intelligence (AI), and Internet of Things (IoT). This is not an inaccurate representation since data science is after all the foundation for ML, AI, and IoT.

Data science is also responsible for creating new processes and methodologies that impact how businesses should be operated today. As a result, data science has led to the spawning of initiatives such as digital transformation and data-driven decision making. Such initiatives change the way organizations solve problems, budget their IT investments, and change the way they interact with customers and citizens.

However, the true definition of data science is that it is a field of study that uses scientific methods, processes, algorithms, and software to extract knowledge and insights from any type of data (structured, unstructured, or semi-structured). Data science is a combination of statistics and computer science applied to relevant domain knowledge of data in order to predict outcomes. And as the saying goes, the enterprise that can most accurately predict the outcomes will have the utmost advantage over its competitors.

© Julian Soh and Priyanshi Singh 2020
J. Soh and P. Singh, *Data Science Solutions on Azure*,
https://doi.org/10.1007/978-1-4842-6405-8_1

Mindset of the modern enterprise

The modern enterprise is one that can quickly respond to the changing environment. Any organization that has an initiative to leverage the use of data it owns and expand on the (ethical) collection of data it does not have, but would be valuable, is considered a modern enterprise. Most organizations recognize that this is an important transformation they must undertake. The digital transformation we are seeing today involves organizations making data the center of their decision-making processes.

It is useful to evaluate the maturity of an organization as it relates to data. If an organization is spending most of its resources addressing tactical issues instead of being strategic, then the organization is lower on the data maturity model.

Commercial entities

Commercial entities are the earliest adopters of data science. For example, retail and customer data allow commercial entities to mine the information to improve sales. Customer sentiment, taste, and even political and social media data can be used as enriching features to help drive sales strategies.

Using manufacturing as another example, data science is used to optimize manufacturing processes by identifying anomalies and defects, thereby reducing or eliminating factors leading to manufacturing defects.

In healthcare, data science is being used to study cell behavior and diseases to develop cures. During the COVID-19 pandemic, researchers[1] also used data science to analyze social media data in order to identify symptoms in patients, which would enable medical professionals to better diagnose patients who may have the virus.

---

[1]Reference: https://medicalxpress.com/news/2020-08-social-media-covid-long-haulers.html

Government entities

Even though public sector entities are traditionally more conservative and will generally lag the commercial sector in adopting modern technologies, data science is one area where the gap is much narrower, at least in the United States and most developed countries.

This is because government organizations traditionally collect a lot of data, and the data is extremely diverse in nature. Different departments in every state have information of its citizens through all the services the state provides. Multiply that by 50 states plus the information collected by the federal government, that is a lot of data to mine and a lot of knowledge and insight that can be gleaned through data science.

Consumer and personal

The consumer sector is probably the most prolific when it comes to data growth, thanks to IoT devices associated with connected homes, wearable technology, and social media. All these technologies fall under the umbrella of Big Data, which we will discuss in detail in Chapter 6. For now, we just want you to appreciate the vast source of rich data that is being collected on a daily basis that is growing at an *exponential* rate.

One important aspect to also recognize is the blurring of the lines between all the different domains mentioned earlier. For example, with the use of personal assistants (e.g., Siri and Alexa), information and data from each domain are now more blended than ever as we rely on personal assistants to carry out tasks.

Ethics in data science

As seen, data proliferation is occurring in every aspect of our lives – at work, where we shop, what we buy, how we interact with others, our political and social views, our governments, and our homes.

This type of digital revolution happens only once in a while, the last being equivalent to the birth of the Internet, and the birth of personal computing before that. As such, new social and ethical challenges arise, and we must acknowledge and address them accordingly.

Ethics in data science is more commonly known as ethical AI. But before we look at ethical AI, let us first see how some things that were once considered science fiction are no longer fiction. We can get an idea on the ethical challenges based on story lines in science fiction.

Science fiction and reality – a social convergence

Hollywood science fiction movies have played their part in introducing intriguing effects of AI on society in movies like *AI Artificial Intelligence* (2001) and *Minority Report* (2002).

Both movies touch on extreme themes. In *AI Artificial Intelligence*, audiences are left to ponder whether an artificial life form is worthy of the same protections as humans when an artificial child is built to possess emotions. In *Minority Report*, predictions made by AI are enforceable before the actual crime is committed.

As AI makes robots and digital assistants more human, the line between fiction and reality is indeed getting blurred. For example, contributing to Japan's issue of aging population is the generation of *otakus,*[2] men who are in relationships with virtual girlfriends – a concept highly promoted in the anime culture and gaming.

Machine learning, a subset of AI, uses algorithms to build mathematical models based on sample data for training and learning, with the goal of making the most accurate predictions and decisions possible. How confident are we with machine-based decisions? Look around you at the Teslas, IoT devices, and smart homes. The US Navy and Boeing have a highly classified program (code-named CLAWS) to develop AI-powered Orca class fully autonomous submarines that are outfitted with torpedoes, meaning these submarines may be able to make the decision to kill indiscriminately. The obvious ethical question: Should a machine be able to kill without human intervention? The increase in concern regarding the need, or potentially lack thereof, of human intervention in AI decision making has led to the alternative and growing popularity of not calling the acronym AI Artificial Intelligence, but rather Augmented Intelligence.

Note   Another sign of the times is the explosion of fake news. Advancements in AI and machine learning are making it easier to create extremely convincing fake videos, known as deepfake. Experts fear that deepfake videos will create an even larger trust issue in journalism and these videos are also being employed in politics.

---

[2]In 2012, a 35-year-old otaku, who is a school administrator, married his virtual girlfriend named Hatsune Miku. www.techspot.com/news/77385-japanese-man-marries-anime-hologram-hatsune-miku.html

What is ethical AI?

Ethical AI is a study and governance surrounding the use of AI technologies in a way that does not violate human rights and endanger lives. We are not exactly at the point of having to address the rights of robots, so that part is still the domain of science fiction.

The impact of AI on life is so important, and as we rapidly meet and surpass human parity in many areas, religious organizations have played a leading role to proactively address this issue. In February 2020, the Vatican in Rome released a guideline for ethical AI, called "Rome Call for AI Ethics[3]," to which Microsoft is one of the first to sign. Listen to Microsoft President Brad Smith's speech at `https://romecall.org/`.

There are many discussions and representations of what ethical AI means, but the three principles in Rome Call for AI Ethics very succinctly summarize the core concepts – ethics, education, and rights.

Other organizations involved in the design and development of AI are also incorporating the important aspect of ethics. DeepMind is another example of an organization that is not only comprised of scientists, engineers, and researchers in the field of AI but also brings together philosophers and policy experts to form truly interdisciplinary teams to address the broad impact that AI has on society. It is indisputable that there is a need for accountability for the development and use of AI, perhaps more so than any emerging technology in recent history. With backing from large corporations like Google, organizations like DeepMind provides a forum to engage citizens, governments, and corporations to agree on fundamental concepts involving ethics. Find out more at `https://deepmind.com/about/ethics-and-society`.

---

[3]`https://github.com/harris-soh-copeland-puca/docs/blob/master/AI%20 Rome%20Call%20x%20firma_DEF_DEF_.pdf`

Note   "AI-based technology must never be used to exploit people in any way, especially those who are most vulnerable. Instead, it must be used to help people develop their abilities (empowerment/enablement) and to support the planet."

—**The Vatican**

Microsoft AI principles

Microsoft has a site dedicated to the company's AI principles at www.microsoft.com/en-us/ai/responsible-ai and is a leader in the charge to ensure ethics are deeply engrained in the development of AI technologies. The most important aspect of Microsoft's AI principles is that it applies to AI at scale since the technology is built into every service and shared across its entire portfolio. For example, threat patterns gleaned by AI in the Xbox service are shared across other services like Office 365, Azure, and Dynamics in order to better protect the entire cloud services portfolio. Even though Microsoft has an Office of Responsible AI tasked with putting the company's principles into practice, common ethical AI design principles are followed across all groups in the organization, from engineering to marketing.

Note   "An important hallmark of our approach to responsible AI is having [the] ecosystem to operationalize responsible AI across the company, rather than a single organization or individual leading this work."

—**Microsoft**

Microsoft's AI principles revolve around the six key concepts:

- Fairness: AI systems must treat all people fairly and with no bias to age, culture, gender, or national origin.

- Inclusiveness: AI systems must engage and empower everyone, with no bias to age, culture, gender, or national origin.

- Reliability and safety: AI systems should perform reliably and safely.

- Transparency: AI systems should be understandable.

- Privacy and security: AI systems should be secure and protect and respect privacy.

- Accountability: People should be accountable for AI systems.

We dedicated a generous amount of time discussing ethical AI because it is a very important one as the technology evolves. For the rest of this chapter, we will introduce the different AI technologies from Microsoft and look at some use cases. However, where applicable, we will bring up specific ethical and legal considerations as it relates to the services.

Azure Machine Learning

Machine learning is a subset of AI and is the other topic we will cover in detail in Chapters 4 and 5. The advancement in all the cognitive services mentioned in the previous section is based on machine learning and the vast amount of training data that are available.

Machine learning is used to train models to not only recognize or detect but also to predict outcomes and thus help drive decision making. Machine learning is fundamentally based on data science and statistical methods. The amount of data and statistical methods often requires a lot of memory and compute, which is an ideal fit for Azure.

In this section, we will cover the options available in Azure that help data scientists and researchers do their jobs. There are primarily two options – the initial implementation known as Azure Machine Learning Studio (classic) and the more recently released Azure Machine Learning. Figure 1-1 summarizes the differences between the two offerings.

Feature	ML Studio (classic)	Azure Machine Learning
Drag and drop interface	Classic experience	Updated experience - Azure Machine Learning designer (preview) (Requires Enterprise workspace)
Code SDKs	Unsupported	Fully integrated with Azure Machine Learning Python and R SDKs
Experiment	Scalable (10-GB training data limit)	Scale with compute target
Training compute targets	Proprietary compute target. CPU support only	Wide range of customizable training compute targets. Includes GPU and CPU support
Deployment compute targets	Proprietary web service format. not customizable	Wide range of customizable deployment compute targets. Includes GPU and CPU support
ML Pipeline	Not supported	Build flexible. modular pipelines to automate workflows
MLOps	Basic model management and deployment	Entity versioning (model, data. workflows), workflow automation, integration with CICD tooling, and more
Model format	Proprietary format. Studio (classic) only	Multiple supported formats depending on training job type
Automated model training and hyperparameter tuning	Not supported	Supported. Code-first and no-code options.
Data drift detection	Not supported	Supported
Data labeling projects	Not supported	Supported

Figure 1-1. *Comparing Azure Machine Learning and Azure Machine Learning Studio (classic). Source =* `https://docs.microsoft.com/ en-us/azure/machine-learning/overview-what-is-machine-learning-studio`

Azure Machine Learning

Azure Machine Learning is a cloud-based environment for data scientists to train, deploy, automate, manage, and track ML models. It is often used in conjunction with cloud storage such as Azure Blob Storage and Azure Data Lake Storage because of the potentially large amount of data being used in the ML process.

Azure Machine Learning supports all the tools and languages used by data scientists, such as R, Python, and Scala. It also has tools such as Jupyter notebooks and supports open source add-ons such as PyTorch, TensorFlow, scikit-learn, and YOLO. It comes with a web interface called the Azure Machine Learning designer.

Azure Machine Learning supports classical ML, deep learning, as well as supervised and unsupervised learning. Azure Machine Learning also integrates with other Azure services, such as Azure DevOps, to help secure the data scientists' work through source control.

Machine Learning Studio (classic)

Azure Machine Learning Studio (classic) is the initial implementation and ML offering in Azure. It is still available and should not be confused with Azure Machine Learning. See the differences in Figure 1-1 again. Download the Azure Machine Learning Studio (classic) architecture to see all its capabilities at `https://download.microsoft.com/download/C/4/6/ C4606116-522F-428A-BE04-B6D3213E9E52/ml_studio_overview_v1.1.pdf`.

Azure Databricks (Chapters 6 and 7)

Azure Databricks is the native implementation of Databricks in Azure and is provided as a PaaS offering. Azure Databricks provides all the tools and resources that data scientists and researchers need and is jointly managed by Databricks and Microsoft engineers.

Azure Databricks are provisioned as workspaces that contain the customizable compute clusters, the notebooks, datasets, and storage. Users can use Databricks File System (DBFS) or mount external storage like Azure Blob Storage or Azure Data Lake Storage to access data for projects. Azure Databricks notebooks allow users with different skill sets to collaborate because the notebooks support different languages like Python, R, Scala, and Spark SQL. All notebooks can be source controlled using GitHub or Azure DevOps.

To optimize resources and reduce cost, compute clusters in Azure Databricks can be automatically shut down due to inactivity. The default is 120 minutes, but this can be configured as needed. Compute clusters can be customized with the desired libraries needed, such as PyTorch, scikit-learn, and TensorFlow. Compute clusters can be pinned so the customization will be preserved even after the cluster is shut down due to inactivity.

Use cases for Azure Databricks

Azure Databricks is often used to prepare raw data for downstream systems and analysis. It is usually front ended by low-latency ingestion solutions such as IoT hubs or event hubs and other types of storage serving non-streaming data. Figure 1-2 depicts a typical architecture of an enterprise data pipeline architecture with data inputs from different sources (streaming and non-streaming) with Azure Databricks as the data preparation environment before sending the prepared data to downstream datastores.

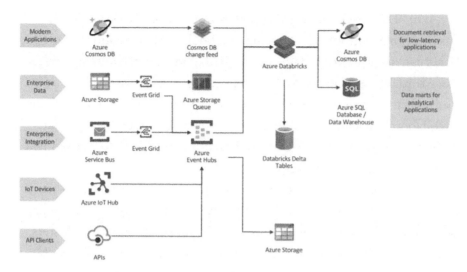

Figure 1-2. *Data ingestion and data manipulation pipeline leveraging Azure Databricks. (Source = https://cloudarchitected. com/2019/03/event-based-analytical-data-processing-with- azure-databricks/)*

You can also read up on two other use cases located at

- https://docs.microsoft.com/en-us/azure/
  architecture/reference-architectures/ai/batch-
  scoring-databricks

- https://docs.microsoft.com/en-us/azure/
  architecture/reference-architectures/data/
  stream-processing-databricks

Summary

In this chapter, we made the case as to why data science is an inevitable undertaking that all modern organizations need to address in order to stay competitive. We also spent some time in understanding new ethical challenges because of AI and ML, which are a result of advancements in data science. Lastly, we provided a quick overview of the modern technologies and tools in Azure that will help data engineers and data scientists conduct their work in a more efficient manner.

CHAPTER 2

Statistical Techniques and Concepts in Data Science

The prominent role that data science plays in technology today has created a need for all professions to possess a strong fundamental working knowledge of the math used in statistical techniques.[1] The "data scientist" today may be a transitioning database professionals, data/Big Data engineers, software engineer, IT auditor, fraud investigator, or even a business analyst. Often, a project team would be comprised of all these professionals that have been brought together to solve a business problem, optimize a process, or create predictive models based on data-driven techniques. It is thus imperative that all members of the team have some idea of the statistical techniques and concepts used in data science.

Whether you are a professional in transition or have a need to get a better understanding of statistical techniques because you are about to embark on a data-driven project, this chapter is designed to help you. If you are a data scientist and do not need a refresher, feel free to skip this

---

[1]Statistical techniques are mathematical concepts, formulas, and equations designed to analyze data so as to identify patterns, make predictions, and understand behaviors.

© Julian Soh and Priyanshi Singh 2020
J. Soh and P. Singh, *Data Science Solutions on Azure*,
https://doi.org/10.1007/978-1-4842-6405-8_2

chapter. In this chapter, we will focus on statistical concepts and using a spreadsheet (Microsoft Excel or equivalent) as a readily accessible analysis tool.

The fundamentals

Data science, as implied by its name, is based on data, and it is up to us to organize and make sense of the data. One of the first tasks when approaching a data-driven project is to ask for all the data that is available, their sources, build data pipelines if necessary, and start understanding the data. Future steps would include cleaning the data, creating your hypothesis, and then conducting experiments to test and validate the hypothesis before finally creating, debugging, deploying, and monitoring a model.

Inputs and outputs

We need to determine the "cause-effect" nature of the data we receive. So, the core fundamental is to determine the inputs (causes) that would influence the outputs (effects).

In data science, inputs can be referred to by different names, such as predictors, variables (or independent variables), and features. Outputs are also sometimes referred to as responses, dependent variables, or simply as results.

In mathematics, inputs are traditionally denoted with the symbol X, and outputs are denoted using the symbol Y. Subscripts are used to denote and identify multiple inputs and outputs, for example, $X_1, X_2, X_3, \ldots X_i$ and $Y_1, Y_2, Y_3, \ldots Y_i$.

Lab setup

All lab and learning resources for this book are hosted on GitHub. We will also be using open datasets primarily found on Kaggle, which we will replicate to the book's GitHub repository (repo).

To better understand the concepts in this chapter, we will use these resources:

- Bank marketing dataset[2] located at `https://github.com/priya-julian/AzureDataScience/blob/master/datasets/Bank%20Marketing%20Dataset/4471_6849_bundle_archive.zip` (original source: `www.kaggle.com/janiobachmann/bank-marketing-dataset`).

- Microsoft Excel version 2010 and up.

- In the Options ➤ Add-ins section for Microsoft Excel, activate the Analysis ToolPak and Solver Add-in.

- Download the free Real Statistics Resource Pack from `www.real-statistics.com/free-download/real-statistics-resource-pack/`, and follow the installation instructions located at this site.

Download the dataset from our GitHub repo or from Kaggle, and unzip the CSV file. We will use this file later in the chapter as we explore the fundamentals and concepts.

---

[2]This is the classic marketing bank dataset uploaded originally in the UCI Machine Learning Repository. The dataset gives you information about a marketing campaign of a financial institution in which you will have to analyze in order to find ways to look for future strategies in order to improve future marketing campaigns for the bank.

Note   If you want to view the completed hands-on exercises in this chapter, please use the bank_solution.xlsx workbook that is also located in our GitHub repo at `https://github.com/singh-soh/ AzureDataScience/blob/master/Chapter02_Statistical_ Techniques_and_Concepts_In_Data_Science/bank_ solution.xlsx`.

Hands-on exercise: Understanding inputs, outputs, and simple modeling

In this exercise, we will explore the concept of inputs and outputs using the bank marketing dataset.

1.   Open the bank.csv file and explore the columns.

2.   Take note of the columns titled "marital," "age," and "balance."

3.   Taking these three columns into consideration and creating a scatterplot in a spreadsheet software like Microsoft Excel, we should get a chart like Figure 2-1.

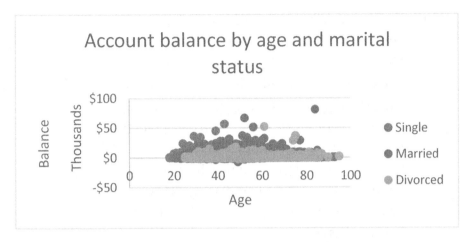

Figure 2-1. *Account balance by age and marital status*

4. What can we tell from the chart? It looks like people who are single and below the age of 40 generally have a higher balance than their peers who are married or divorced. It also shows that people wo are divorced generally have a lower balance compared to their peers, which makes sense since divorced individuals generally have to split assets and maintain separate households.

    Therefore, we can represent a relationship between the outputs Y (balance) and inputs X (age). The marital status serve as predictors, *p*, and can be denoted as $X_1, X_2, X_3,...,X_p$. In this example, X_1 = Single, X_2 = Married, and X_3 = Divorced.

5. This relationships can then be represented as

$$Y_{balance} = (X_{age}) + \epsilon$$

    where *f* is a function of X, in this case the age, and ϵ is an error term which is independent of X.

6. Let's separate the individuals by marital status
    and analyze their bank balance based on age.
    Figures 2-2, 2-3, and 2-4 show the prediction of the
    bank balance (Y) of individuals based on their age
    (X) and a function (f) of their marital status. By
    using the least squares fit for each data point (also
    known as linear regression), we can create a simple
    model of predicting the trend of the bank balance
    for the different groups based on age. This analysis
    approach using least squares fit is also known as
    linear regression.

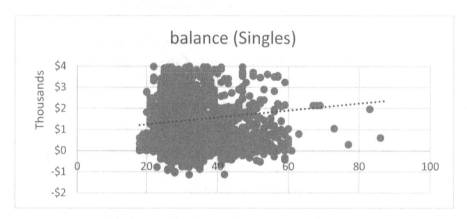

Figure 2-2. *Bank balance for singles with simple least squares*

Figure 2-3. *Bank balance for married individuals with simple least squares*

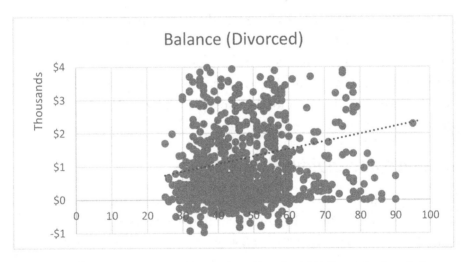

Figure 2-4. *Bank balance for divorced individuals with simple least squares*

Prediction and inference

In data science and statistical learning, our goal is to derive the function f as accurately as possible. Having derived f, we can then use the model for prediction or inference.

Prediction

Prediction is when we use known inputs, X, and using the derived function f, predict the output Y.

In many cases, inputs are readily available, and the task at hand is to predict the outcomes. Using our bank dataset example, now that we have estimated the impact of one's marital status (f) on the bank balance, for any given age, we can take the person's marital status into consideration and predict what the balance of their bank account might be.

In this scenario, users of this model may not care about the *how* the marital status function f impacts the bank account balance, but rather is more interested about predicting what that balance may be. Therefore, f can be treated as black box for the users of the model. This is a classic prediction exercise.

Inference and multivariate analysis

Inference is when the user of a model actually needs to understand *how* the function f affects the outcome Y for specific input(s) X. In this scenario, f cannot be treated as a black box.

As an example, let us say that one of the bank's clients is changing their marital status from single to married. We may want to determine *how much* that may impact the individual's bank account balance, not just predicting what that balance may be. Being able to do so may allow us to provide financial planning advice and services for this individual.

A common use of inference is when there are multiple inputs that affect the output, and we need to determine how much impact each of the inputs has on the output. We can organize our data analysis based on the number of inputs that may affect an output. A multivariate analysis is one that has multiple inputs, while a bivariate analysis is one that specifically has two inputs, although this is often called a multivariate analysis as well. A univariate analysis is one that only has one input.

As an example, looking at the bank dataset again, assume we are tasked with designing products and services for our clients. We would have to take several factors into consideration. The more factors we take into consideration, the more targeted and relevant our services would be.

With that in mind, we can add "age" and "education" as inputs[3] that can potentially impact the bank account balance (output). Knowing the bank account balance should give us an idea on how much clients can invest or the types of services and products we can offer.

We can visualize the data in three dimensions. Figures 2-5, 2-6, and 2-7 are surface plot charts showing the average account balances of individuals in their 20s, 30s, and 40s with their education level added as a third dimension.

In Figure 2-5, we see that education level has a big impact on the account balance for individuals between the age of 20 and 22. Individuals with just a primary education have a much higher account balance than individuals with a tertiary education level. This is likely because individuals are paying off student loans or are in the process of getting a tertiary education and thus not saving or working as much. As an inference problem, we want to understand how, why, and how much the education level affects individuals between 20 and 22 years of age. Between the ages of 25 and 29, there is a complete reversal in the average balance for individuals with primary education vs. those with tertiary education.

---

[3]In data science, inputs are usually referred to as features.

Likewise, in Figure 2-7, for individuals in their 40s, we see that education level is a more significant input than age. While there may be fluctuations in the bank account balance by age, the chart clearly shows a consistent difference between those individuals with primary level education and those with tertiary education. Therefore, we may focus on designing two types of services for clients in their 40s. One would be catered to those with primary education and another for those with tertiary education.

Finally, in Figure 2-6, we see that there is a spike in the average balance for individuals between 33 and 35, and their level of education is less of a factor affecting the balance. As an inference problem, we seek to understand the reasons affecting those in this age bracket, and this may lead us to design products and services catered to these individuals, with the likely marketing campaign not taking education level into consideration.

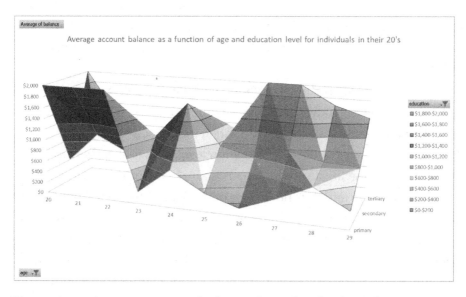

Figure 2-5. *Average account balance for individuals in their 20s as a function of their age and education level*

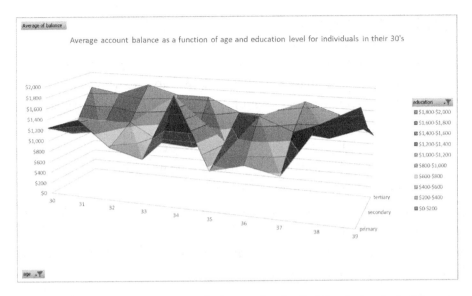

Figure 2-6. *Average account balance for individuals in their 30s as a function of their age and education level*

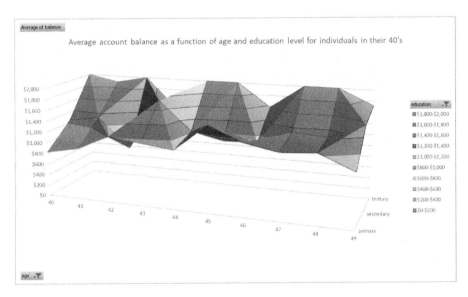

Figure 2-7. *Average account balance for individuals in their 40s as a function of their age and education level*

Machine learning

Now that we have a better understanding on inputs, outputs, and basic modeling techniques using Microsoft Excel, we can use the observed data to train a model in order to handle prediction and inference use case scenarios as mentioned in the previous section.

Machine learning is an AI technique where we use software to train a model using relevant and observed data. In the preceding example, we have identified relevant data from the bank dataset to be the age, balance, and education level for the use cases we are interested in. The model that is trained with the observed data can then be used to make predictions for new/unknown cases. In mathematical terms, we are going to use machine learning as a technique to derive f.

Deriving f through machine learning

Delving into the math of deriving f is beyond the scope of this book. Instead, we will look at how we use machine learning to derive f through a practical look at use case scenarios.

Refer again to the chart in Figure 2-7, and consider this use case. We need to design a new service for our bank customers. As part of designing the new service, we need to determine what is affordable to customers, and a good indicator of that is their average monthly balance. The chart in Figure 2-7 provides us with the visual representation of customers' average balance based on their age and education level.

Hands-on exercise: Exploring bank dataset

In this exercise, we will open the bank.xlsx workbook and explore the dataset:

1. Download and open bank.xlsx from our GitHub repository (`https://github.com/singh-soh-gollob/AzureDataScience/blob/master/Chapter02_Statistical_Techniques_and_Concepts_In_Data_Science/bank.xlsx`).

2. Navigate to the worksheet named "age-education-balance."

3. We modeled a surface plots for adults by 5-year age groups (20, 25, 30, 35,…65) and their average bank balance relative to their education as shown in Figure 2-8.

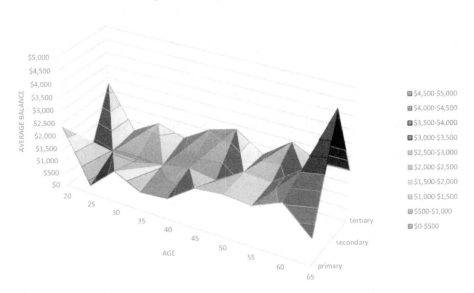

Figure 2-8. *Average balance by 5-year age groups and education level*

4. If we take age as an input and call it X_1 and education level as a second input and call it X_2, then we can define a function for the average balance:

$$f[X_1, X_2] = [Y]$$

5. In data science, strings are not very useful, so we will represent[4] primary education level as 1, secondary education level as 2, and tertiary education level as 3. This is seen in the column headers in the second pivot table in the spreadsheet and as shown in Figure 2-9.

Average of balance	Column Labels			
Age	1	2	3	Grand Total
20		$2,375	$408	$2,764	$998
25		$334	$960	$1,109	$968
30		$1,238	$943	$1,699	$1,276
35		$728	$1,037	$1,397	$1,165
40		$827	$1,249	$2,028	$1,410
45		$1,565	$1,086	$2,338	$1,525
50		$1,683	$1,728	$1,660	$1,698
55		$1,592	$1,669	$2,443	$1,884
60		$2,067	$2,459	$1,947	$2,234
65		$1,066	$4,944	$1,978	$2,952
Grand Total		$1,348	$1,284	$1,750	$1,452

Figure 2-9. Replace education level with numeric values

---

[4]In data science, we use numeric values for all our analysis. Therefore, we should convert all string values into a numeric representation. This is called encoding.

6. Look for the row of the pivot table for 20-year-olds, and let us call this data point 1. We will represent this as

$$f[X_{11}, X_{21}] = [Y_{11}]$$

where X_{11} is our first observed input data point, which is the age group input for an individual, and X_{21} is our second observed input data point, which is the education level input for a 20-year-old. Therefore, the observed output data point (balance) for a person in this demographic, Y_{11}, is \$2,375.

7. Expanding the observed data points for a 20-year-old,

$$f[X_{11}, X_{22}] = [Y_{12}]$$
$$f[X_{11}, X_{23}] = [Y_{13}]$$

where X_{22} is the education input for a 20-year-old with secondary education that has an observed output ($Y_{12} = \$408$) and finally X_{23} is the education input for a 20-year-old with tertiary education that has an observed output ($Y_{23} = \$2,764$), so on and so forth.

8. Putting it all together, we can write the following relationship:

$$f[X_{11}, X_{21}] = [Y_{11}]$$
$$f[X_{11}, X_{22}] = [Y_{12}]$$
$$f[X_{11}, X_{23}] = [Y_{13}]$$
$$f[X_{12}, X_{21}] = [Y_{21}]$$
$$f[X_{12}, X_{22}] = [Y_{22}]$$
$$f[X_{12}, X_{23}] = [Y_{23}]$$
$$f[X_{13}, X_{31}] = [Y_{31}]$$

$$f[X_{13}, X_{32}] = [Y_{32}]$$
$$f[X_{13}, X_{33}] = [Y_{33}]$$

$$\cdots$$

$$[X_{1i}, X_{ij}] = [Y_{ij}]$$

where

$f[X_{11}, X_{21}] = [Y_{11}]$	20-year-old, primary education with observed average balance of \$2,375
$f[X_{11}, X_{22}] = [Y_{12}]$	20-year-old, secondary education with observed average balance of \$408
$f[X_{11}, X_{23}] = [Y_{13}]$	20-year-old, tertiary education with observed average balance of \$2,794
$f[X_{12}, X_{21}] = [Y_{21}]$	25-year-old, primary education with observed average balance of \$334
$f[X_{12}, X_{22}] = [Y_{22}]$	25-year-old, secondary education with observed average balance of \$960
$f[X_{12}, X_{23}] = [Y_{23}]$	25-year-old, tertiary education with observed average balance of \$1,109
$f[X_{13}, X_{31}] = [Y_{31}]$	30-year-old, primary education with observed average balance of \$1,238
$f[X_{13}, X_{32}] = [Y_{32}]$	30-year-old, secondary education with observed average balance of \$943
$f[X_{13}, X_{33}] = [Y_{33}]$	30-year-old, tertiary education with observed average balance of \$1,699
$f[X_{1i}, X_{ij}] = [Y_{ij}]$	i is the ith observed age group and j is a value between 1 and 3 to indicate whether it is primary, secondary, or tertiary education level for the observed age group

9. For the sake of this exercise, even though we have data for every age group, let us assume that we only have the observations for 5-year age groups, $[X_1]$ = [20, 25, 30, 35, 40, 45, 50, 55, 60, 65].

10. When a model is successfully trained, an unknown data point can then be fed to the model, and it should be able to predict the average balance for this age group, for example, a 42-year-old individual with secondary education (X_i = 42 and X_2 = 2). Figure 2-10 depicts this data point with our model.

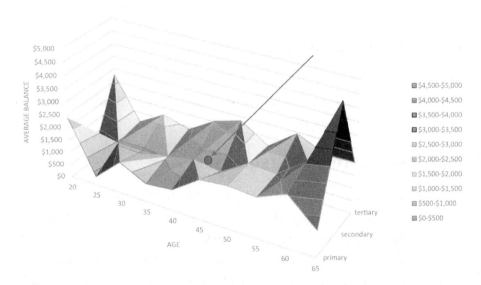

Figure 2-10. *Depicting a 42-year-old with secondary education with our model*

31

Types of machine learning

The main types of machine learning are supervised and unsupervised learning. However, there are four types of machine learning:

1. Supervised learning

2. Unsupervised learning

3. Semi-supervised learning

4. Reinforcement learning

We are going to cover only first and second machine learning types in this book, while the third and fourth machine learning types will not be covered.

Supervised learning

Supervised learning is a technique where we use observed/known data to train a model. There are essentially two types of supervised learning – regression and classification.

Supervised learning by regression

With regression,[5] we use most of the known data to train a model but withhold a certain percentage of the data for testing purposes. After the model has been developed, the test data is fed to the model, and the predicted results (also known as scored labels or just labels) are then compared to the actual known results (also known as actual labels). This

---

[5]Regression is a statistical method used to determine the strength and relationship between a dependent variable (output) and one or more independent variables (inputs). Two basic types of regression are univariate linear regression and multivariate linear regression. There are also nonlinear regression methods for more complicated data analysis.

will tell us the accuracy of the prediction and therefore the performance of the model. Generally, 70% of a dataset is used for training purposes, and 30% is withheld for testing.

As an example, consider the data for 30-year-old individuals where we would like to take a more granular look at how their education level impacts their average balance. Instead of just 1, 2, and 3 being the numeric representation of the level of education, we included fractional levels where, for example, 2.5 may indicate individuals who have post secondary education but have not acquired tertiary education. These would include individuals that may have an associate degree instead of a bachelor's degree.

Taking *some*, not all, of the observed data (reserve a portion for testing), we plot that information as shown in Figure 2-11.

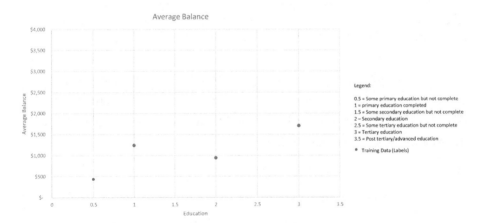

Figure 2-11. *Data points using training data in supervised learning*

When subjected to supervised machine learning using regression, we attempt to fit a model f as shown in Figure 2-12. Let us consider this as our first attempt (epoch[6] 1).

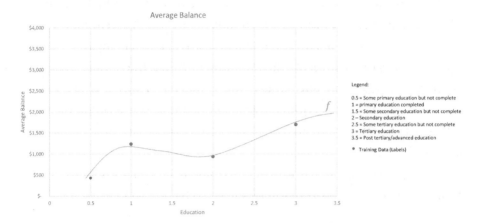

Figure 2-12. *Model derived based on training data in supervised machine learning (epoch 1)*

Next, we will use the data that was withheld to test it against the derived model. The difference between the scored label and the actual label is called the residual, and it is used to determine the level of error in the model, as shown in Figure 2-13.

---

[6]Epoch is a commonly used term in data science to identify a particular time-marked event. In these next series of exercises, we will use epoch to identify the different iterations of an experiment.

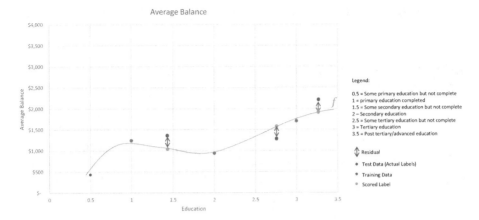

Figure 2-13. *Testing the performance of the model using test data and residual values (epoch 1)*

Determining the level of error in *f*

Since the level of error in a model determines the performance of a model, and hence whether we ultimately accept or reject the model, we need to understand the basics on measuring the error in the model using the residual values.

There are two types of error measurements – absolute vs. relative.

Absolute measures

There are two ways to calculate absolute errors in a model – Root Mean Squared Error (RMSE) and Mean Absolute Error (MAE).

Root Mean Squared Error (RMSE)

$$\text{RMSE} = \frac{1}{n}\sqrt{(\sum_{i=1}^{n}(\text{Score}_i - \text{Label}_i)^2}$$

Using the three data points in Figure 2-11 (epoch 1), we can derive Table 2-1.

Table 2-1. *Score vs. label values to derive the residual (epoch 1).*

$n = 3$ Epoch = 1	n_1 (Education ~1.5)	n_2 (Education ~2.75)	n_3 (Education ~3.25)
Score	1050	1550	1900
Label	1400	1250	2250
Residual (score – label)	-350	300	-350
Absolute residual value|(score – label)|	350	300	350

Therefore,

$$\text{RMSE}_{\text{epoch1}} = \frac{1}{3}\sqrt{((1050-1400)^2+(1550-1250)^2+(1900-2250)^2)}$$

$$= \frac{1}{3}\sqrt{(335000)}$$

$$= 193 [7]$$

Now, assume that by collecting more data points and using machine learning, we were able to get a smoother and more accurate fit for f by retraining our model, and let us call this epoch 2. Table 2-2 shows a possible scenario of data from epoch 2.

---

[7]The unit of RMSE and MAE is the same as the unit of the outcome Y, in this case, $. Although RMSE and MAE are often represented without units, they are not dimensionless.

Note With machine learning, it is common to train a model many times using more/different data until we get a well-performing model. Tracking the performance of models is an important exercise, and we will introduce this in Chapter 4.

Table 2-2. *Score vs. label values to derive the residual (epoch 2).*

$n = 3$ Epoch = 2	n_1 (Education ~1.5)	n_2 (Education ~2.75)	n_3 (Education ~3.25)
Score	1325	1331	2125
Label	1400	1250	2250
Residual (score – label)	-75	81	-125
Absolute residual value|(score – label)|	75	81	125

Now,

$$\text{RMSE}_{\text{epoch2}} = \frac{1}{3}\sqrt{((-75)^2 + (81)^2 + (-125)^2)}$$

$$= \frac{1}{3}\sqrt{(27811)}$$

$$= 56$$

Comparing RMSE from both epochs, the model from epoch 2 performs better because its error level is lower. Therefore, we accept the model generated in epoch 2 and reject the model from epoch 1.

Mean Absolute Error (MAE)

$$\text{MAE} = \frac{1}{n}\sum_{i=1}^{n}|score - label|_{1} \text{ where } n = number\ of\ errors$$

Referring to Tables 2-1 and 2-2 again, we calculate MAE with n = 3 since there are three error points:

$$\text{MAE}_{\text{epoch1}} = \frac{1}{3}\Sigma(350 + 300 + 350)$$
$$= 333$$

$$\text{MAE}_{\text{epcoh2}} = \frac{1}{3}\Sigma(75 + 81 + 125)$$
$$= 94$$

We arrive at the same conclusion using MAE that the model in epoch 2 performs better.

RMSE vs. MAE

Both RMSE and MAE are commonly used to measure accuracy, although RMSE is a more popular model and is frequently the default modeling metric. A deeper mathematical analysis of RMSE vs. MAE is beyond the scope of this book, but will be a useful topic for you to explore. But for now, just know that RMSE tends to increase more than MAE when there are large errors. In other words, you observe a high frequency of smaller residual values occurring in the model, and then either RMSE or MAE can be used. However, if you observe any high residual values in the model, RMSE gives more weight to such errors.

Relative measures

The units of absolute measures can sometimes be problematic. Using our earlier examples for $RMSE_{epoch\,2}$, is $56 a big or small error? Well, ±$56 is a small error if it is compared against $1,000, but will be a big error if it is $100.

To address this challenge, we use relative measures to get a better sense of the error level. Relative measures represent errors as a dimensionless value between 0 and 1, where a value closer to 0 represents the better model.

Two types of relative measures are Relative Absolute Error (RAE) and Relative Squared Error (RSE).

Relative Absolute Error (RAE)

$$RAE = \frac{\sum_{i=1}^{n}|Score - Label|}{\sum_{i=1}^{n}(Label)}$$

Using Table 2-2 from epoch 2,

$$RAE_{epoch2} = \frac{|(-75+81-125)|}{(1400+1250+2250)}$$

$$= \frac{119}{4900}$$

$$= 0.024$$

Let us imagine we ran a third training session with more and/or different data points and got the following results shown in Table 2-3.

Table 2-3. *Score vs. label values to derive the residual (epoch 3).*

n = 3 Epoch = 3	n_1 (Education ~1.5)	n_2 (Education ~2.75)	n_3 (Education ~3.25)
Score	1327	1338	2105
Label	1400	1250	2250
Residual (score − label)	-73	88	-145
Absolute residual value|(score − label)|	73	88	145

Using Table 2-3 from epoch 3,

$$\text{RAE}_{epoch3} = \frac{(-73 + 88 - 145)}{(1400 + 1250 + 2250)}$$

$$= \frac{130}{4900}$$

$$= 0.027$$

Comparing RAE_{epoch2} and RAE_{epoch3}, we can see that model 3 performs marginally worse than model 2. We would not have been able to tell easily if we used RMSE or MAE.

Relative Squared Error (RSE)

$$\text{RSE} = \sqrt{\left(\frac{\sum_{i=1}^{n} (Score - Label)^2}{\sum_{i=1}^{n} (Label)^2} \right)}$$

Therefore,

$$RSE_{epoch2} = \sqrt{\left(\frac{(-75)^2 + (81)^2 + (-125)^2}{1400^2 + 1250^2 + 2250^2} \right)}$$

$$= \sqrt{\frac{27811}{8585000}}$$

$$= 0.057$$

$$RSE_{epoch3} = \sqrt{\left(\frac{(-73)^2 + (88)^2 + (-145)^2}{1400^2 + 1250^2 + 2250^2} \right)}$$

$$= \sqrt{\frac{34098}{8585000}}$$

$$= 0.063$$

RSE also shows that epoch 3 does not perform better than epoch 2.

Supervised learning by classification

Another type of supervised learning is via a technique called classification. With this technique, we can predict which category something or someone belongs to.

Looking at our bank account balance dataset, personal information such as age, job, marital status, and education level can be used to develop a model that can classify whether a person will likely default.

Unlike regression, where the output is a numeric value, classification is generally a binary problem. In our example, we seek a "yes" or "no" answer to whether a client is likely to default.

Hands-on exercise: Classification

In this exercise, we will explore concepts of supervised learning to address a classification problem:

1. Open the bank.xlsx workbook, and select the spreadsheet named "age-job-marital-edu-default."

2. Note that we have selected only the fields that we feel will affect the state of default for a client, as partially shown in the left table in Figure 2-14. This process is known as feature engineering. Selecting the right features is usually based on understanding the data. Good candidates for features are also values that are measured or collected directly and not calculated or derived.

	A	B	C	D	E		G	H	I	J	K
1	age	job	marital	education	default		age	job	marital	education	default
215	44	managem	divorced	tertiary	yes		44	4	2	3	1
216	32	techniciar	single	secondary	no		32	2	0	2	0
217	31	unemploy	married	secondary	no		31	8	1	2	0
218	40	self-empl	married	secondary	yes		40	10	1	2	1
219	43	entrepren	married	secondary	no		43	7	1	2	0
220	27	managem	single	secondary	no		27	4	0	2	0
221	37	services	single	secondary	no		37	3	0	2	0
222	23	services	single	secondary	no		23	3	0	2	0
223	25	managem	married	primary	no		25	4	1	1	0
224	26	blue-colla	single	secondary	yes		26	6	0	2	1

Figure 2-14. *Age, job, marital status, and education as a function of default*

3. As before, when doing statistical analysis and machine learning, it is better to convert strings into numbers. Look at the legend to see the values we have selected to represent the marital status, job, and education level of a client. These are then used to replace the string values, as partially shown in the right table in Figure 2-14.

4. From our data, we can identify individuals that are in default or not. Looking at the individuals in rows 215 through 224 (refer to the spreadsheet or in Figure 2-14), we can use machine learning to define a binary classifier function f as such:

$$([X_{age}, X_{job}, X_{marital}, X_{education}]) = Y[1/0]$$
$$([44,4,2,3]) = 1$$
$$([32,2,0,2]) = 0$$
$$([31,8,1,2]) = 0$$
$$([40,10,1,2]) = 1$$
$$([43,7,1,2]) = 0$$
$$([27,4,0,2]) = 0$$
$$...$$

True/false positives, true/false negatives

The binary function f will not actually calculate a number 0 or 1, but rather a number between 0 and 1. So each data point will fall within that range, and if we take 0.5 as a default mid-point threshold, we can visualize a classification chart like the one shown in Figure 2-15.

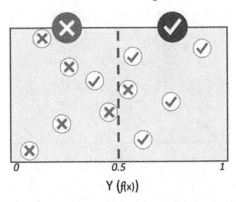

Figure 2-15. *Classification chart with threshold 0.5*

Remember that classification is a form of supervised learning, so the approach we take would be similar whereby a portion of the observed data is used to train the classification function f and a subset of the observed data is reserved to test the performance of f.

Using an initial threshold of 0.5, we assume that every data point to the left of the threshold should be a negative and everything to the right is a positive. In other words, we assume that if we use the inputs for an individual and their data point is less than 0.5, then they are not likely to default. Whereas if their data point is greater than 0.5, then they are likely to default.

During testing, if the predicted value for a data point is positive and the actual value is also positive, then this is known as a true positive (TP).

If the predicted value for a data point is positive, but the actual value is negative, then this is a false positive (FP).

Similarly, if a predicted value for a data point is negative and the actual value is also negative, then this is a true negative (TN). Finally, if the predicted value for a data point is negative, but the actual value is positive, then this is a false negative (FN).

Data points that are FP or FN are misclassified, and often, data points that are very close to the threshold can get misclassified, as shown in the revised chart in Figure 2-16.

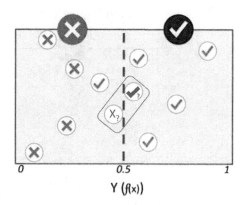

Figure 2-16. *Possible misclassification of data points close to the threshold*

We can set the threshold to be more conservative by moving it to the left, or more aggressive by moving it to the right. Moving it to the left may result in higher false positives (FP) but reduce false negatives (FN), maybe even down to zero. Figure 2-17 depicts the result if we reduce our threshold.

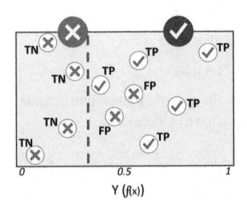

Figure 2-17. *Lowering the threshold*

In our use case scenario, minimizing the number of false negatives at the expense of having more false positives may not be a bad thing. This means that the likelihood of us incorrectly predicting a client not defaulting is minimized, which reduces the bank's risk profile. We may lose some potential business by not offering our new financial product (e.g., a new credit card offer) to a client who was incorrectly identified as being likely to default (FP). But that may be better than having more clients that default because we incorrectly offered the new product to them.

Evaluating performance of classification model

The performance of a classification model is the variance between predicted outcomes and actual outcomes.

Confusion matrix

The TP, TN, FP, and FN of a model can be tabulated into a 2x2 matrix. For example, if we tabulate the results of and get something like this

Number of TP = 500

Number of TN = 300

Number of FP = 10

Number of FN = 30

We can represent the preceding tabulation in a matrix, called a confusion matrix, as shown in Figure 2-18.

Predicted \ Actual	1	0
1	500	10
0	50	300

Figure 2-18. *Confusion matrix*

Accuracy

One way of evaluating the performance of a classification model is to determine its accuracy. Accuracy is simply the number of correctly classified cases.

$$
\begin{aligned}
\text{Accuracy} &= \frac{(TP + TN)}{(TP + FP + TN + FN)} \\
&= \frac{(500 + 300)}{(500 + 10 + 300 + 50)} \\
&= 0.93 \text{ (or 93\%)}
\end{aligned}
$$

At first glance, an accuracy of 93% sounds like a pretty good performing model. However, a more meaningful way of evaluating the performance of a classification model is to use precision and recall.

Precision

Precision is defined as the number of correctly classified positives. Therefore, precision is a metric that focuses on how well a model is correctly identifying TP.

$$\text{Precision} = \frac{TP}{(TP + FP)}$$

Using the confusion matrix in Figure 2-18 to calculate the precision of this classification model

$$\text{Precision} = \frac{500}{(500 + 10)}$$

$$= 0.98 \text{ (or 98\%)}$$

This means that 98% of cases where we identified a client who may default will indeed default. And 2% of the clients will not go into default.

Recall

In some cases, we may want a metric that focuses on the fraction of positive cases we correctly identify, and this is known as the recall, or sometimes also referred to as the true positive rate (TPR). In our use case, recall is a better metric because we want to know how well we are identifying clients who may default.

$$\text{Recall} = \frac{TP}{(TP + FN)}$$

$$= \frac{500}{(500 + 50)}$$

$$= 0.91 \text{ (or 91\%)}$$

About 91% may not be an acceptable risk level, because it is better if we can achieve a recall that is close to 100%. That would mean that we identified all the cases where clients go into default.

So, if we moved the threshold and would result in the following confusion matrix as shown in Figure 2-19, where the number of FN decreases but the number of FP increases, then

$$\text{Recall} = \frac{TP}{\left(TP + FN\right)}$$
$$= \frac{547}{\left(547 + 3\right)}$$
$$= 0.99 \, (\text{or } 99\%)$$

and

$$\text{Precision} = \frac{547}{\left(547 + 84\right)}$$
$$= 0.87 \, (\text{or } 87\%)$$

$$\text{Accuracy} = \frac{\left(547 + 300\right)}{\left(547 + 84 + 3 + 300\right)}$$
$$= 0.91 \, (\text{or } 91\%)$$

Predicted \ Actual	1	0
1	547	84
0	3	300

Figure 2-19. Confusion matrix (epoch 2)

Both our precision and accuracy went down, but our recall significantly improved. Depending on your use case scenario, you may want a higher recall, or you may want a higher precision.

For example, as mentioned earlier, to minimize the bank's exposure to risk, we desire a higher recall since that would maximize correctly identifying all cases where a client may default.

False positive rate (FPR)

Remember that the recall is also known as TPR. There is a related metric to the TPR known as the false positive rate (FPR).

$$\text{FPR} = \frac{FP}{(FP + TN)}$$

Referring to the confusion matrix in Figure 2-19,

$$\text{FPR} = \frac{84}{(84 + 300)}$$
$$= 0.22 \text{ (or 22\%)}$$

$$\text{TPR} = \text{Recall} = \frac{547}{(547 + 3)} = 0.99 \text{ (or 99\%)}$$

Receiver operating characteristic (ROC) curve

A ROC curve is a graphical plot of FPR (x axis) against TPR (y axis) and serves as a visual representation of the performance of a binary classification function.

Hands-on exercise: Plotting the ROC curve

To plot the ROC curve, we need to move the threshold and determine the TP, TN, FP, and FN based on the threshold. Then calculate the FPR and TPR and finally plot the curve.

1. Open bank.xlsx.

2. Click the spreadsheet named "ROC."

3. Based on the three classification charts, note the values for TP, TN, FP, and FN. The first two charts identify the actual values (rows 5 and 8). The third chart does not explicitly identify the actual values for TP, TN, FP, and FN but determines those yourself and compare your values to what we have provided in row 10.

4. Optional: Determine what the FPR and TPR could be if the threshold is moved to the extreme left (0.1 and row 4).

5. Optional: Find the TP, TN, FP, and FN for other threshold values.

6. Note the points for a ROC curve that can be plotted from the calculated FPR and TPR values.

7. Plot the ROC curve as shown in Figure 2-20.

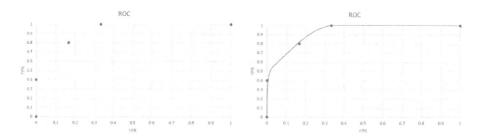

Figure 2-20. *Plotting the ROC curve*

8. Note that this is the classic shape of a ROC curve.

9. The area under curve (AUC), as shown in
    Figure 2-21, represents how well the classification
    function performs. The larger the AUC, the better
    the performance.

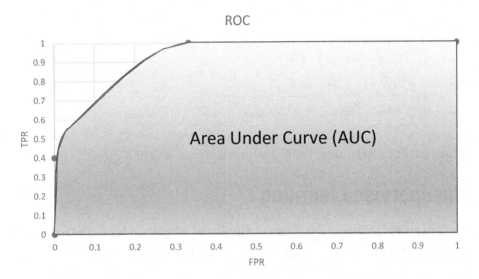

Figure 2-21. *Area under curve of the ROC*

10. On a ROC graph, a 50-50 guess is simply represented
    by a diagonal line that intersects (0,0) and (1,1) as
    shown in Figure 2-22.

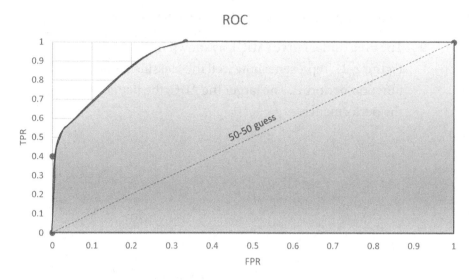

Figure 2-22. *AUC and ROC performance vs. a 50-50 guess*

Unsupervised learning

Unsupervised learning is a method employed when you have no known data that you can use for training a model. A type[8] of unsupervised learning is a technique called clustering.

Clustering

With clustering, we group data points into clusters based on observed similarities. There are several types of clustering techniques, such as K-means, mean-shift clustering, density-based spatial clustering of applications with noise (DBSCAN), agglomerative hierarchical clustering, and so on. For this exercise, we will look at K-means clustering.

---

[8]Two main types of unsupervised learning are principal component and cluster analysis.

52

For example, if we select about 100 individuals with just their age and balance as inputs from our bank dataset and plot them on a scatter chart, we will get a chart like the one shown in Figure 2-23. Mentally, picture how the data points can be grouped into clusters.

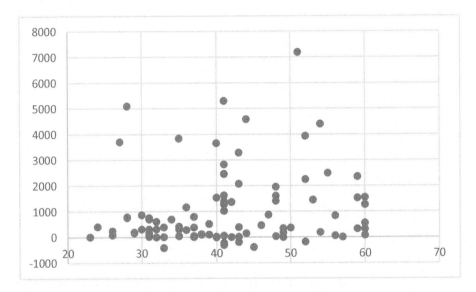

Figure 2-23. *Scatterplot of age-balance from 100 clients*

K-means clustering

A popular technique for clustering is one called K-means clustering. With K-means clustering, we decide the number of clusters we want to create. Clusters are denoted by the symbol k. So, if we want 3 clusters, then k = 3.

We plot k points (centroids) randomly but evenly distributed so we can group data points around them, thus forming well-defined clusters, as shown in Figure 2-24.

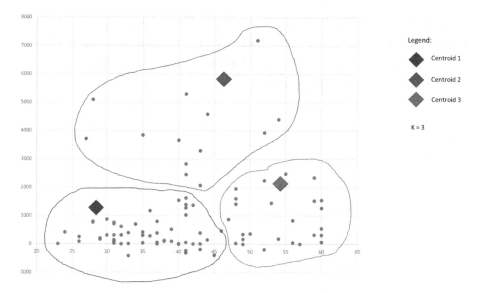

Figure 2-24. *Initial grouping of k clusters around randomly placed centroids*

Next, we find new location for the centroids by calculating the mean values of the points distance to derive a point that is in the middle of all the data points. The centroids are then relocated to the true center of all the points in the respective clusters and then redefine the clusters based on the new location of the centroids, as shown in Figures 2-25 and 2-26.

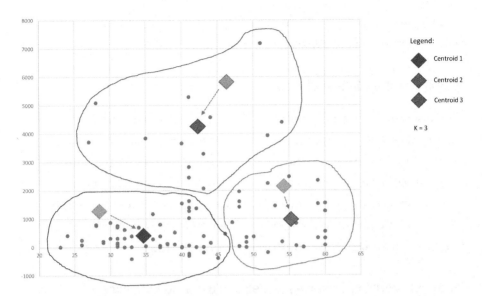

Figure 2-25. *Relocating the centroids to the true center of the points within the cluster*

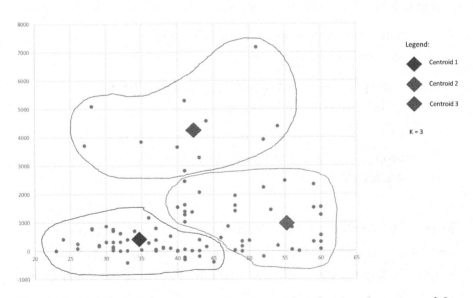

Figure 2-26. *Redefining the clusters based on the new location of the centroids*

This process constitutes an iteration, and we repeat this process until we have optimized the separation of the clusters.

Optimized separation of clusters

What does an optimized separation of the clusters mean? When an optimized cluster separation is achieved, this means that the clusters have separated the data by the greatest extent possible. To measure cluster separation optimization, we take the average distance between the centroids from each other and compare that to the average distance between all the points in the cluster to their respective centroids. Clusters that have maximized this ratio are considered optimized.

Hands-on exercise: Exploring K-means clustering with Excel

In this hands-on exercise, we will use the Real Statistics Resource Pack for Excel and the bank dataset to explore and understand K-means clustering.

1. Open bank.xlsx workbook, and select the spreadsheet titled "Clustering."

2. This spreadsheet is a sampling of the first 500 rows of data from the bank dataset.

3. Click Add-ins from the Excel menu, and click the drop-down menu for Real Statistics, and select Data Analysis Tool.

Note   If you do not see the Add-ins menu, use CTRL-M to bring up Real Statistics. Visit www.real-statistics.com/appendix/faqs/disappearing-addins-ribbon/ to troubleshoot this issue.

---

4. From the Real Statistics dialog box, select the tab called "Multivar," and click K-Means Cluster Analysis. Then click OK.

5. Click the Input Range box, and then select all the data in rows 1 to 501 and columns A and B.

6. Make sure the "Column headings included with data" check box is checked.

7. For the parameters, accept 3 as the number of clusters, but change the number of iterations to 10.

8. Click the Output Range text box (it may have A1 as a value) and type C1.

Note   If you leave the Output Range box blank, the results from the analysis will be placed in a new spreadsheet within the same workbook. In some scenarios, this can be useful, for example, if you are going to rerun the analysis with a different number of iteration and have the results from each run in its own spreadsheet.

---

9. Click OK.

10. Depending on your computer,[9] this may take some time (but should not be more than a couple of minutes; it took about 4 minutes for me to do 100 iterations).

---

[9]The computer used in this exercise was an Intel Core i7 10th generation CPU with 16GB or RAM.

age	balance	C	Cluster		Centroid	1	2		3		1	2	3	Dist-sq
59	2343	1	1		age	41.36111	39.81818		38.20863309		1082113	45475773	3754436	1082113
56	45	2	3		balance	3383.097	9086.545		405.4748201		11143107	81749806	130258.6	130258.6
41	1270	3	3								4465180	61098384	747411.6	747411.6
55	2476	4	1		k		3				823011.4	43699542	4287356	823011.4
54	184	5	3								10234383	79255517	49300.46	49300.46
42	0	6	3		iter		50				11445347	82565313	164424.2	164424.2
56	830	7	3								6518520	68170805	180538.2	180538.2
60	545	8	3		SSE		2.68E+08				8055143	72958406	19942.14	19942.14
37	1	9	3								11438601	82547144	163601.3	163601.3
28	5090	10	1								2913696	15972515	21944880	2913696
38	100	11	3								10778739	80758003	93314.91	93314.91
30	309	12	3								9450203	77045401	9374.773	9374.773
29	199	13	3								10138628	78988581	42716.65	42716.65
46	460	14	3								8544519	74417325	3033.701	3033.701
31	703	15	3								7183028	70283912	88573.2	88573.2
35	3837	16	1								206068.2	27557751	11775375	206068.2
32	611	17	3								7684611	71834932	42279.15	42279.15
49	-8	18	3								11499599	82710841	171077.9	171077.9
41	55	19	3								11076231	81568815	122840.4	122840.4
49	168	20	3								10336909	79540537	56510.74	56510.74

Figure 2-27. *Partial screenshot of the K-means analysis results*

11. The important information we want from the analysis result is the column titled Cluster. To the left of that column is just the line number, so we can remove it. There should be 500 rows with values since that was our data input.

12. Select the entire Cluster column, right-click, and then choose Paste Special.

13. Select Values and click OK.

Note   We need to do this because we cannot sort the data by clusters since this column contains a formula. Therefore, we need to convert it to value first.

---

14. Delete column C.

15. Sort the data by the Cluster column in ascending order.

16. Now plot a scatter chart using (as shown in Figure 2-28)

   a. age as the x-axis

   b. balance as the y-axis

   c. Cluster as the series data

   d. Centroid 1 (age and balance) as a separate series

   e. Centroid 2 (age and balance) as a separate series

   f. Centroid 3 (age and balance) as a separate series

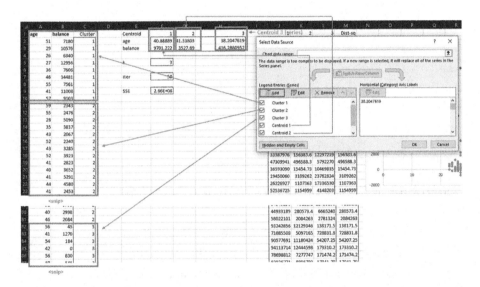

Figure 2-28. Plotting clusters and centroid on a scatter chart

17. Optional: Locate the centroids and change their size, shape, and color so they are easier to identify. As an example, in Figure 2-29, we changed the centroids to red, size to 10, and border to black.

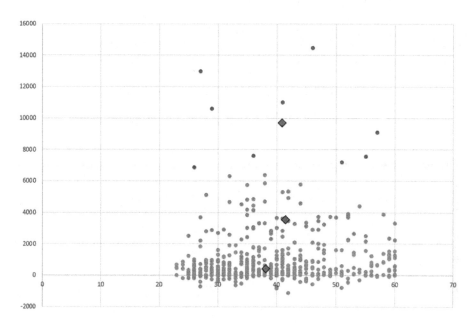

Figure 2-29. *Clusters and centroids on a scatter chart*

18. We can now visually identify the clusters with respect to the centroids. Figure 2-30 shows the completed and labeled K-means cluster (clusters were drawn manually).

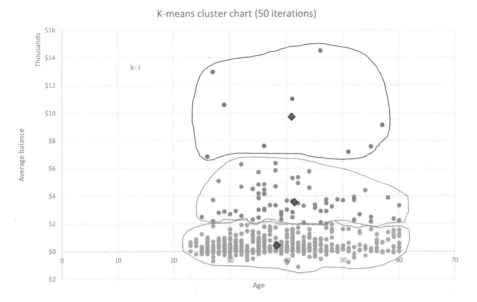

Figure 2-30. *Identifying the clusters*

Closing thoughts and optional exercises

1. Explore distance data generated by the analysis and how that can be used to determine the optimization of the cluster separation.

2. Run additional analysis with higher (or lower) number of iterations. Do you observe any changes in the cluster separation?

Causation and correlation

Causation and correlation are very similar and deceptively difficult to discern. However, the ability to determine which is which will help with experiment design and maximize the effectiveness of your data-driven decisions.

Causation describes a direct cause-and-effect relationship between two or more random entities. For example, an action A leads to an outcome B, or in other words, action A causes outcome B.

Correlation is when two random events are observed together, but they may or may not be *directly related*. For example, action A and action B are related, but action A does not necessarily cause action B to occur (or vice versa).

Use case: Problem diagnosis

Every time mobile app A is launched (action A), it crashes the phone (outcome B). It may seem that A causes B. However, upon further diagnosis, the issue is a result when there is insufficient memory on the phone (case C). When there is sufficient available memory, for example, fewer other applications are running, action A succeeds. Therefore

1. A is correlated to B.

2. C causes B when A is introduced.

Before we embark on a potentially expensive and time-consuming effort to redesign the application, we should investigate whether we have data for phone usage or types of phone subscribers own. We can then set up experiments to determine if there is a high or low probability of issue 2 occurring. If it is low, then a workaround can be implemented instead of an expensive redesign (e.g., as simple as informing phone user that there is insufficient memory and instructions on how to free up more memory).

Experiment design

Understanding and being able to identify causation vs. correlation is important when designing our experiments. We use this information to identify inputs, outputs, and our hypothesis. We then run tests to prove or disprove our hypothesis.

The goal is to definitively identify causation through rigorous testing. We will discuss experiment design using methods such as hypothesis testing and A/B/n experiments later in this book and also at our GitHub repo located at `https://github.com/singh-soh/AzureDataScience`.

Summary

This chapter was written primarily for new and aspiring data scientists. We have only extracted the core data science and statistical principals that are foundational and will be applied in later chapters. Please visit our GitHub repo for more resources and reference materials.

In this chapter, we went through the core statistical concepts that data scientists use. We visited regression and classification techniques as part of supervised machine learning. We also covered performance metrics which can be used to decide which model performs better. As part of unsupervised machine learning, we touched upon clustering technique and particularly K-means clustering in detail. We also went through many hands-on exercises which would have given you enough insights to understand some basic statistical techniques which are widely used in data science projects.

## CHAPTER 3

Data Preparation and Data Engineering Basics

There is a common saying that the bulk of the work involved with data science is in data preparation. In fact, data preparation is a crucial part of the process, which, if not done correctly, would yield inaccurate results and may lead to negative consequences. That is why so much time is being spent on data preparation. If we want to make the data science process more efficient, shaving off the amount of time spent on data preparation is one area for us to look at.

However, we need to qualify what we mean by "shaving off the amount of time spent in data preparation." It does not mean we spend less time on it by reducing the attention to detail dedicated to data preparation. What it means is that we need to find a way to make the preparation process more efficient by using modern tools, technologies, and processes.

In this chapter, we will look at the core tools that aid in making data preparation more efficient. The data preparation stage is also known as data engineering, and many organizations are starting to pay special attention in this area. In fact, most organizations now have data engineers on staff to help get data prepared, cleaned, and ready for the data scientists.

© Julian Soh and Priyanshi Singh 2020
J. Soh and P. Singh, *Data Science Solutions on Azure*,
https://doi.org/10.1007/978-1-4842-6405-8_3

What is data preparation?

Let us use our bank data as an example. In Chapter 2, we presented a scenario where the bank may want to design a new investment product that is catered to certain demographics. For example, this new product is catered to people with a certain level of disposable income or the potential of achieving that level within the next 3 to 5 years.

Knowing the potential of a bank's customer, and therefore the potential size of the clientele, we would need to conduct an analysis to determine the demographics that will qualify for this new product. Demographics, in this case, would include information like job, age, balance, marital status, and education level.

The rest of the columns like loan, housing, contact, campaign, and so on may not be relevant, so we should remove them. However, we may need to enrich the data from other sources as well (e.g., address) so that we can take other factors into consideration in our analysis.

Finally, nulls in columns may throw off our analysis, so we may want to remove rows or normalize numeric columns with averages.

This is an example of data preparation, and all the work is designed with one goal in mind – making the analysis as accurate and as relevant as possible.

Note   About 50% of data scientists surveyed[1] site data quality and cleanliness as one of their top three challenges in their job.

---

[1]www.datasciencetech.institute/wp-content/uploads/2018/08/Data-Scientist-Report.pdf.

The challenge of data preparation

A survey conducted by Figure Eight Inc. (CrowdFlower[2]) found that data scientists spend

- 60% of their time gathering and cleaning data

- 19% of their time on collecting datasets

- 9% of their time data mining and understanding the data and patterns

- 3% of their time training the datasets

- 4% of their time refining algorithms

- 5% of their time spent on other tasks

From the preceding survey, we conclude that on average, data scientists spend only 16% of their time doing actual data science work (9% + 3% + 4%).

The task of cleaning and preparing data is where data scientists spend the bulk of their time. The survey also revealed that this is the part of the job that most data scientists (57%) viewed the least glamorous and enjoyable part of their job. Furthermore, 19% of the data scientists surveyed consider collecting datasets as the least enjoyable task.

As discussed in Chapter 6, the characteristics of Big Data are a significant factor in driving the complexity of data preparation. To keep up with Big Data and to be able to optimize the time and effort spent on data preparation, modern tools such as Azure Data Lake Services (ADLS Gen2), Azure Blob Storage, Azure Data Factory Pipelines, Azure Machine Learning Pipelines, Azure Synapse Pipelines, and Azure Databricks need to be in the data engineers' toolbox. In fact, it is our opinion that the awareness and ability to use these tools are almost mandatory skills for not just data engineers but also for data scientists.

---

[2]Figure Eight Inc., formerly known as CrowdFlower, is a San Francisco-based company providing AI and solutions for data scientists.

In this chapter, we will be introducing the fundamental building blocks of a data pipeline and the associated technologies and tools.

Modern data pipeline

The modern data pipeline needs to meet the following criteria:

- A central, limitless, and flexible storage solution that can accommodate structure, unstructured, and semi-structured data

- A data orchestration solution for scheduling jobs and defining the steps involving data movement, consolidation, and manipulation in a secure fashion

- An advanced data transformation and cleaning solution

Figure 3-1 is an example of a modern data pipeline. In this chapter, we will focus on the data engineering aspects of the data pipeline, and as such, we will take a closer look at the services in the data ingestion and transformation phases.

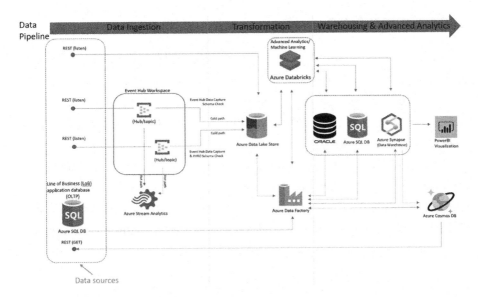

Figure 3-1. *Modern data pipeline architecture*

Data ingestion – Sources

Referring to Figure 3-1, on the far left of the architecture diagram are examples of data sources.

In most real-world scenarios, data sources can be, and often are, transactional databases supporting Line of Business (LoB) applications. Due to the growing number of IoT devices, more and more data are also being streamed in through REST endpoints.

There are multiple Azure services that can serve as ingestion points, and in Figure 3-1, Azure Event Hub[3] and Azure SQL Databases (or traditional OLTP databases) are represented as examples of traditional data sources.

---

[3]Azure Event Hub is one of the several serverless message bus services. Other serverless Azure messaging services include IoT Hub, Event Grid, and Queues.

Transformation

Data transformation includes the copying of data from data sources as well as any needed transformation. Transformation includes activities such as data cleaning and enriching (joins/merges between disparate sources). Transformation generally occurs after loading and hence the term extract, load, transform (ELT[4]).

Therefore, before transformation can take place, a common landing spot for raw data needs to be established. The Azure architectural blueprint for the data science life cycle identifies storage accounts (Azure Blob or Azure Data Lake Store, ADLS) as the ideal candidate for raw and staging data prior to being loaded into data warehouses.

Azure Blob Storage

Azure Blob Storage is the most economical and abundant storage that is available today. It derives its name from the term BLOB, which stands for Binary Large Objects, although it is usually represented in all lower case.

The definition of a blob is a large file, typically an image or any form of unstructured data. We will talk about the different data types in Chapter 7, but for now, think of blobs as large files that are not suited to reside in databases. The hard drive on your personal computer can be considered a blob storage because it houses different types and sizes of files that are organized in folders.

---

[4]It is increasingly popular to carry out data pipeline activities in the extract, load, transform (ELT) sequence as opposed to the more traditional extract, transform, load (ETL) because it is more efficient to do so and to take advantage of modern technologies such as Polybase loads.

The big difference between the storage on your personal computer and blob storage in Azure is that

- Azure Blob Storage is infinitely scalable and virtually limitless.

- Azure Blob Storage is physically backed by at least three sets of infrastructure – from drives to power supplies. This is the default deployment and is known as locally redundant storage (LRS). LRS is the minimal deployment model. See Figure 3-1.

- Azure Blob Storage can also be replicated to a remotely paired data center in Azure, which will also be another three sets of infrastructure in that remote location. This is known as geo-redundant storage (GRS). Therefore, in a GRS configuration, data is being replicated across six sets of hardware spanning two geo-locations more than 500 miles apart.

- Azure Blob Storage is the least expensive type of storage in Azure. To provide some context, at the time of writing, Azure Blob Storage prices are $0.03/GB/month[5] for the hot tier and as little as $0.01/GB/month for the archive tier. This pricing is competitive among cloud providers, and Microsoft has demonstrated the willingness to continue making the price of storage competitive. Azure Blob Storage should be considered enterprise-level storage, so it is economical to provision cloud storage in Azure than maintain on-premises hardware.

---

[5]Azure workload prices may change, and different regions may have different prices. Prices mentioned in this book are to provide context and should not be assumed accurate.

There are two types of Azure Blob Storage:

- Block Blob: Block Blob Storage is ideal for files up to 200GB in size. Block Blob Storage is normally used for unstructured data of varying sizes, such as videos, photos, and other binary files.

- Page Blob: Page Blob Storage is optimized to hold files that are used for random read and write operations. Therefore, they are often used to store the virtual hard disk (vhd) images of virtual machines in Azure.

To read, write, download, and upload files to Azure Blob Storage, HTTPS PUT and GET methods are employed. To facilitate that, Azure provides public URL endpoints to access Azure Blob Storage, although recently, Microsoft announced the Private Link service, which would allow a public endpoint in Azure to be exposed with a privately owned IP address. Azure Private Link is discussed elsewhere in this book.

The URL to access blob storage in Azure is usually a .blob.core. windows.net suffix. Therefore, to access a blob stored in a container of a storage account will look something like this:

https://<Storage AccountName>.blob.core.windows. net/<ContainerName>/<BlobName>

For more detailed information about Azure Blob Storage, we have forked Microsoft's extensive and evergreen documentation for Azure Blob Storage to our GitHub repo located at `https://github.com/singh-soh/ azure-docs/blob/master/articles/storage/blobs/storage-blobs- overview.md`.

Hands-on: Deploying Azure Blob Storage

In this exercise, we will be deploying an Azure Storage Account in order to then deploy Azure Blob Storage. We will then explore how we would transfer files to and from Azure Blob Storage and how to secure it.

As we start the deployment process, remember the relationship of the storage account to the blob containers and blobs, as seen in Figure 3-2.

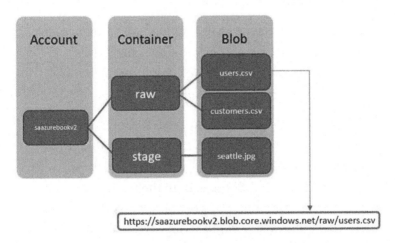

Figure 3-2. *Structure and relationship of the storage account, blob containers, and blobs*

As with all the other hands-on exercises, we will assume that you have an Azure subscription, or know to sign up for a free trial:

1. Go to your Azure portal at https://portal.azure.com and sign in.

2. Click Create a resource and type storage account in the search box. Select Storage account – blob, file, table, and queue when it appears in the search results.

3. Click Create.

4. Select the subscription to put the storage account in, or create a new subscription for it.

5. Provide a name for the storage account. The name is used as part of the URL endpoint, so it must be globally unique. It must also be in lowercase and no special characters.

6. Select a location closest to you.

7. Select a performance level. Standard performance will be backed by high-performance enterprise-level hard disk drives. Premium performance will be backed by enterprise-level solid-state drives.

8. Leave the Account kind at StorageV2. StorageV2 accounts are recommended for almost all storage scenarios and incorporate all the functionality of StorageV1 and BlobStorage. Both these storage types are still mainly provided for backward compatibility, for example, if there is a need to access the storage account using the classic model rather than the Azure Resource Manager (ARM) method. See `https://docs.microsoft.com/en-us/azure/storage/common/storage-account-overview#recommendations` for more details.

9. For this exercise, leave the access tier (default) as hot, unless we know for sure that this storage account is generally used for files that can tolerate some latency like near-line access. Blobs that are uploaded to this storage account will be assigned this tier by default, and we can move the blob to hot or archive tier after the upload.

10. Click Next: Networking.

11. Select Public endpoint (all networks), and then click Next: Advanced.

12. Keep the Secure transfer required option set to Enabled to enforce HTTPS communication at all times.

13. Large file shares is disabled because we did not pick Premium as the storage type in step 7. Large file shares, if enabled, will allow us to create file shares that are up to 100 TiB in size.

14. Leave Blob soft delete disabled. We can enable soft delete for additional protection against accidental deletes. The duration that deleted blobs are preserved if soft delete is enabled is based on the retention period, which we would specify if we enabled this feature.

15. Leave Data Lake Storage Gen2 Hierarchical namespace (HNS) disabled because we are not deploying Azure Data Lake Services with this storage account. If we enabled Hierarchical namespace, it would also mean we are specifying this storage account as an Azure Data Lake Store account so we will not be able to deploy other storage types to this storage account.

16. Click Review + create.

17. Click Create.

18. After the storage account is deployed, click Go to resource.

We have just deployed an Azure Storage Account, but we have not deployed Azure Blob Storage, or any storage type for that matter. In the following steps, we will deploy Azure Blob Storage by specifying the first container:

1. Go to the Overview pane of the Azure Storage Account we created in the previous exercise if you are not already there.

2. Select Containers in the Overview pane, as seen in Figure 3-3.

Figure 3-3. *Containers (Blob) option in Azure Storage Account*

3. Click + Container located at the top of the pane.

4. Type "raw" for the container name. We will be using this container for the Data Factory hands-on exercise later in this chapter.

5. Leave the Public access level as Private (no anonymous access).

6. Click OK.

7. Click + Container again and create another container with the name "stage."

8. Your Azure Storage Account with Azure Blob Storage should now look similar to what is shown in Figure 3-4.

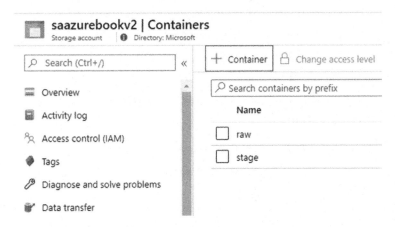

Figure 3-4. *Azure Blob Storage with two containers deployed*

We have now deployed Azure Blob Storage. Next, we will need to store and retrieve files.

Hands-on: Using Azure Blob Storage

As part of this exercise, we will be downloading some content and using Azure Storage Explorer to upload the content to Azure Blob Storage. We will then confirm the content is properly uploaded.

1. Download the bank dataset from `https://
    github.com/singh-soh/AzureDataScience/
    blob/master/datasets/Bank%20Marketing%20
    Dataset/4471_6849_bundle_archive.zip`.

2. Extract the bank.csv file from the downloaded
    zip archive.

3. Download Azure Storage Explorer from https://azure.microsoft.com/is-is/features/storage-explorer/, and install it on your computer. This will be the application we will be using to upload, download, delete, and browse containers and blobs in Azure Blob Storage.

4. Go to the Azure portal and open the Azure Storage Account that we created in the previous exercise.

5. Click Access keys under Settings.

6. Just take note of the Storage account name. Then copy the connection string associated with key1, as seen in Figure 3-5.

Figure 3-5. *Storage account connection string*

7. Launch Azure Storage Explorer.

8. Click the Connect icon and select Use a connection string, as seen in Figure 3-6. Then click Next.

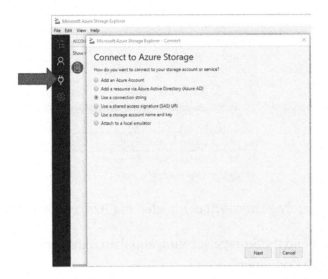

Figure 3-6. *Use a connection string to connect to Azure Blob Storage*

9. Paste the connection string we copied in step 6 into the Connection string field. Notice that the Display name will automatically be populated with the Azure Storage Account name, as noted from step 6. We will leave it like this, but you can change it if desired. This will just be the display name in Azure Storage Explorer. Click Next.

10. Click Connect.

11. Upon successful connection, we should see the storage account listed under Local & Attached ➤ Storage Accounts, as seen in Figure 3-7.

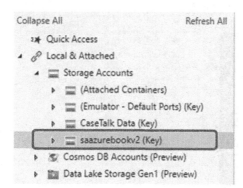

Figure 3-7. Storage account connected via Azure Storage Explorer

12. Expand the Storage account, and then right-click the Blob Containers.

13. Select Create Blob Container, and create a container named "raw."

14. Repeat steps 12 and 13 to create another container named "stage."

Self-guided exercises

The user interface (UI) of Azure Storage Explorer is very intuitive. If you have used any SFTP or FTP client before, this will be no different. Try these exercises on your own.

1. Expand the Storage Account, and then expand Blob Containers. You should see the two containers we created in the previous exercise.

2. Upload bank.csv to the container named "raw."

3. Look for folder statistics, and see the activity history under Activities.

4. Try connecting to the Storage Account using a storage account name and a key instead of a connection string.

5. Try connecting to the Storage Account by adding an Azure subscription and not using a key.

6. Check out Storage Explorer from the Azure portal (in preview at the time of this writing).

7. Create an empty folder. (See the following note.)

Note   Blobs stored in Azure Blob Storage are stored in a flat system. The names of "folders" that blobs are stored in are basically part of the blob's filename. Therefore, if there are no files in a folder, the folder cannot exist. That is why when you try to create a folder, Azure Storage Explorer reminds you that folders are virtual in Azure Blob Storage. Read the next section on Hierarchical namespace (HNS) support in Azure Data Lake Store.

Next steps: Azure Blob Storage

Microsoft's documentation on Azure Blob Storage can be found on GitHub at `https://github.com/singh-soh/azure-docs/tree/master/articles/storage/blobs`.

Azure Data Lake Store (ADLS)

Closely related to Azure Blob[6] Storage is the Azure Data Lake Store. Azure Data Lake Store is the only service that cannot share an Azure Storage Account with the other Azure storage options discussed in this chapter.

Azure Data Lake Store covered in this book will be in reference to the second generation of the service, often called Azure Data Lake Store Gen2 or ADLS Gen2.

Azure Data Lake Store Gen 2 is built on Azure Blob with a few differentiating features, such as

- ADLS Gen2 is better suited for certain scenarios involving analytics because it works better with text files than Azure Blob (applies to analytics involving text files and not video, of course).

- ADLS Gen2 supports Hierarchical namespace (HNS) support. Hierarchical namespace support is essentially the ability to have a folder structure that is independent of the content, meaning we can now have empty folders!

- ADLS Gen2 costs more than Azure Blob Storage and does not have an archive tier.

- ADLS Gen2 supports the assignment of credential-/ role-based access control to folders.

Provisioning an Azure Data Lake Store follows the same steps as deploying an Azure Storage Account with the exception that in the Advanced tab of the provisioning process, enable Hierarchical namespace, as seen in Figure 3-8.

---

[6]In fact, ADLS is built on top of Azure Blob Storage. ADLS Gen2 is a set of capabilities dedicated to Big Data analytics.

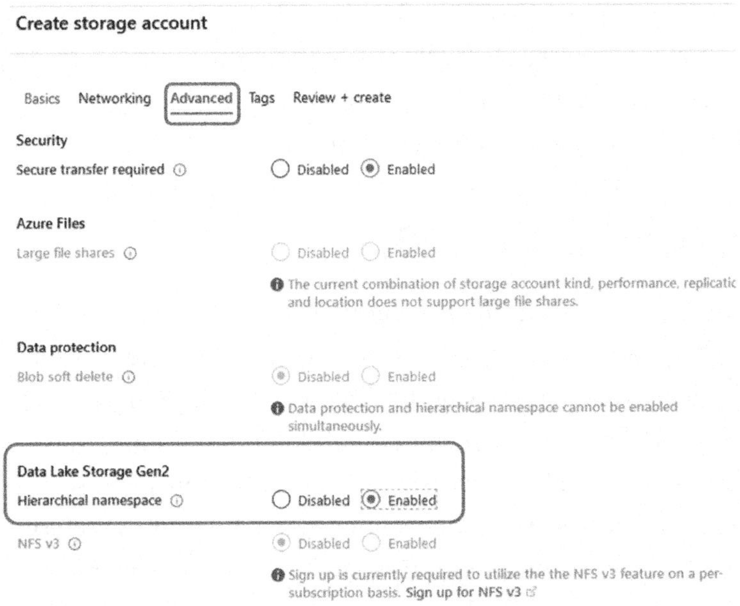

Create storage account

Basics   Networking   Advanced   Tags   Review + create

Security

Secure transfer required ⓘ   ○ Disabled ⊙ Enabled

Azure Files

Large file shares ⓘ   ○ Disabled ○ Enabled

ⓘ The current combination of storage account kind, performance, replicatic and location does not support large file shares.

Data protection

Blob soft delete ⓘ   ⊙ Disabled ○ Enabled

ⓘ Data protection and hierarchical namespace cannot be enabled simultaneously.

Data Lake Storage Gen2

Hierarchical namespace ⓘ   ○ Disabled ⊙ Enabled

NFS v3 ⓘ   ⊙ Disabled ○ Enabled

ⓘ Sign up is currently required to utilize the the NFS v3 feature on a per-subscription basis. **Sign up for NFS v3** ⌖

Figure 3-8. *Provisioning ADLS Gen2 by specifying HNS*

For more information regarding Azure Data Lake Store, please see the Microsoft documentation on this topic at our GitHub repo located at `https://github.com/singh-soh/azure-docs/tree/master/articles/ data-lake-store`.

Data orchestration

Data orchestration occurs throughout the modern data pipeline and is generally defined as the steps involved in copying/moving data from location to location and taking care of any data transformation that needs to occur in the sequence.

The term "pipeline" in modern data pipeline derives its name from the steps that need to occur as data is being ingested, transformed, and then moved or copied from one location to another. The order of those steps, their dependencies, and the identification or sources and destinations is known as data orchestration.

Azure Data Factory (ADF) is a feature-rich Azure service dedicated to data orchestration, and as we will see later, the core functionality in ADF is its ability to efficiently enable data engineers and data scientists design, execute, automate, and monitor data pipelines.

Azure Data Factory (ADF)

Azure Data Factory is a PaaS data orchestrator. The main use case for Azure Data Factory is being the single tool to manage all data estate management activities, such as moving, copying, loading, and transforming data. Azure Data Factory comes with many on-premises and cloud connectors to different types of data sources and applications to unlock the data within those sources. Like everything else, the best way to better understand Azure Data Factory is to get our hands dirty with some hands-on exercises. We will start with an exercise to deploy Azure Data Factory and explore its interface and capabilities. Then we will do more exercises based on a few use case scenarios.

We have also forked a copy of Microsoft's documentation for Azure Data Factory to our GitHub repo located at `https://github.com/singh-soh/azure-docs/tree/master/articles/data-factory`.

Hands-on: Provisioning Azure Data Factory

In this first exercise, we will deploy an instance of Azure Data Factory and explore its user interface (UI) and some of Azure Data Factory's capabilities:

1. From the Azure portal, click Create a resource.

2. Type Data Factory in the search box, and click Data Factory in the search results.

3. Click Create.

4. Give this instance of Azure Data Factory a globally unique name.

5. Keep V2 as the version to deploy.

6. Place this Azure Data Factory in an existing resource group or create a new one.

7. Pick a location closest to you.

8. Click Next: Git Configuration, and check the box titled "Configure Git Later."

Note   Git is a source and change control technology that can be used to protect the artifacts in Azure Data Factory, such as pipelines, datasets, connections, and so on. It is highly recommended that you turn on Git even though this is beyond the scope of this book.[7]

---

9. Click Create.

10. After Azure Data Factory is created, click Go to resource.

For Azure Data Factory, the core user interface is the hosted authoring tool. There is no software to install, and you will spend most of your time in the authoring tool.

Hands-on: Exploring Azure Data Factory

In this exercise, we will explore the authoring workspace of Azure Data Factory. This workspace is the core of Azure Data Factory and is the place where data engineers will spend most of their time.

---

[7]A similar exercise is also outlined in our other book that does go into details of integrating Git as a part of DevOps. Please refer to www.apress.com/us/book/9781484259573.

1. From the Overview pane of Azure Data Factory,
   locate and click Author and monitor. This will
   launch Azure Data Factory authoring workspace.

Note   Instead of going to the Azure portal, selecting the Azure Data
Factory instance, then clicking Author and monitor, you can also
go directly to the Azure Data Factory author workspace by going to
https://adf.azure.com. If you have multiple subscriptions and/
or Azure Data Factory instances, you will be given the opportunity to
select the correct subscription and Azure Data Factory instance.

---

2. From the left border, locate and click the pencil
   icon, which will launch the authoring UI, as seen in
   Figure 3-9.

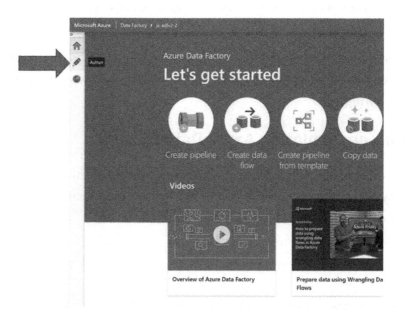

Figure 3-9. *Authoring in Azure Data Factory*

3. When the authoring workspace is launched, locate the five different classes of Azure Data Factory resources – pipelines, datasets, data flows, connections, and triggers, as seen in Figure 3-10.[8]

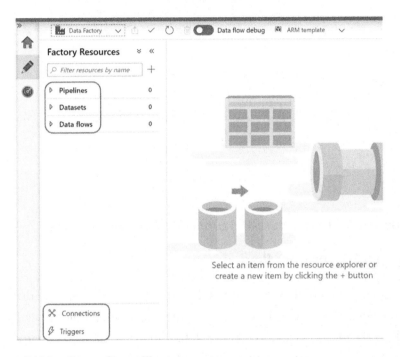

Figure 3-10. *Azure Data Factory resources*

Let us take a moment to explore these Azure Data Factory resources. These resources are the elements we use to build a data pipeline activity. Using these resources via the UI is a matter of dragging and dropping them onto the canvas to the right, or by clicking + located next to the search box. Figure 3-11 depicts the relationship between the Azure Data Factory resources and how they are used as building blocks.

---

[8]As of September 2020, Connections and Triggers as seen in Figure 3-10 was removed and are now located within Datasets and Pipelines, respectively.

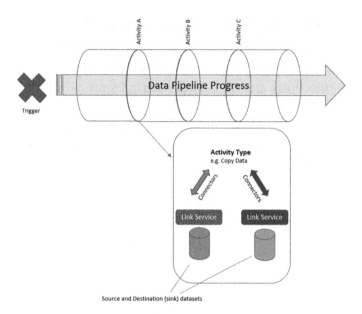

Figure 3-11. *Architecture of Azure Data Factory resources*

Data pipeline or data flow

The data pipeline or flow represents the orchestration work to be done by Azure Data Factory. It describes the sequence in which different activities need to take place in order to get the data into the right form and location. Figure 3-12 overlays the representation of the data pipeline onto how an actual pipeline may look like in Azure Data Factory. In the figure, each of the boxes represents an actual Azure Data Factory activity that is carried out in sequence from the left to the right. Each activity has dependencies from the previous activity and may take parameters as inputs to control the workflow.

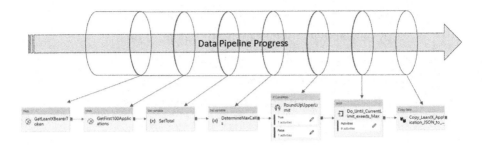

Figure 3-12. *The data pipeline/flow*

1. Click the + that is located next to the search box in Azure Data Factory's authoring workspace, and select Pipeline, as seen in Figure 3-13.

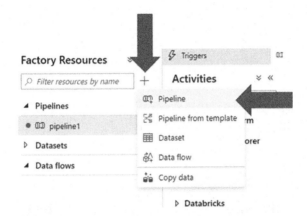

Figure 3-13. *Creating a new pipeline in Azure Data Factory*

2. A new pipeline named pipeline1 will be created and placed under Pipelines.

3. A new pane titled Activities will appear. Explore the different types of activities that a data pipeline can hold.

4. Expand Move & transform and drag and drop the Copy data activity to the canvas for pipeline1 on the right. Then change the name of this activity and see it change in the canvas as well, as seen in Figure 3-14. For this exercise, we will name this activity "Copy_from_Blob_to_Blob."

Figure 3-14. *Copy data activity in Azure Data Factory*

5. Click Code (the {}) at the top right corner of the canvas, and look at the JavaScript Object Notation (JSON) definition for this pipeline. Then click Cancel when you are done.

Triggers

Triggers are quite self-explanatory. Triggers activate the data pipeline process and can be based on schedule, event, or timed intervals (tumbling window).

1. From within the pipeline that we created in the preceding exercise, click Add trigger and select New/Edit.

2. Since we have no existing triggers, click the drop-down in the Choose trigger box and select + New.

3. Observe the properties of the trigger object, as seen in Figure 3-15. Click Cancel for now because we are only exploring the trigger and not actually implementing it.

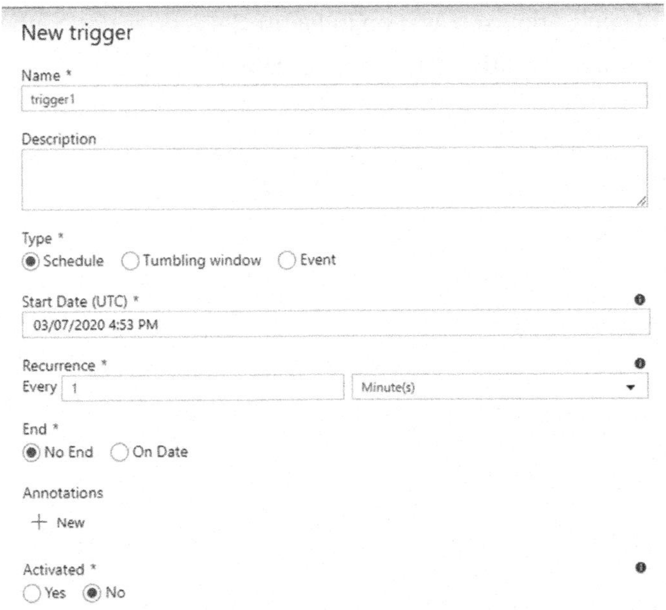

Figure 3-15. *Azure Data Factory trigger options*

Datasets

Datasets are the repositories where data is sourced or deposited. These repositories may be databases such as SQL or Oracle, or they can be from services like a REST API endpoint, or they can be from a SaaS API like SalesForce or Dynamics 365.

Figure 3-16 shows the properties of an Azure SQL Database dataset object in Azure Data Factory. Clicking the different tabs of this dataset object shows the different properties that we would have to set up in order to establish connectivity to the data source and ultimately the content. Each dataset object that is available in Azure Data Factory will consist of unique and known properties that are specific to the data source type. In this example, since the dataset is an Azure SQL Database, its property would contain a field for the table that this dataset object should access. Compare this to the properties of a JSON dataset, which is essentially a file that resides in some location but is generally the format for files received via REST. The properties of such a dataset, as seen in Figure 3-17, does not contain a field to identify a table, but rather a file path and the encoding type.

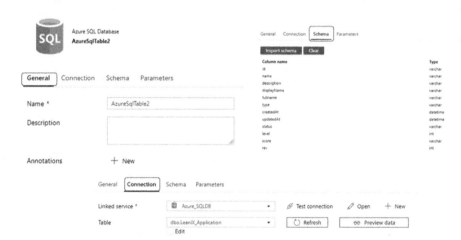

Figure 3-16. *Properties of an Azure SQL Database dataset in Azure Data Factory*

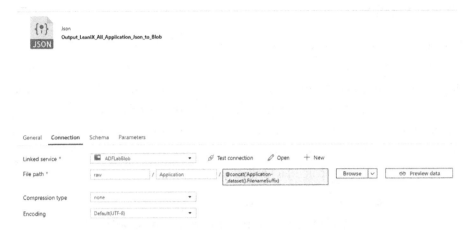

Figure 3-17. *Properties of a JSON file as a dataset*

1. Click the ellipses next to Datasets, and select New dataset.

2. Browse through the different built-in datasets that Azure Data Factory can use. Then click the Azure tab, and select Azure Blob Storage.

3. Click Continue.

4. Select DelimitedText as the format, and then click Continue.

5. Give this Dataset a name. For this exercise, we will use the name CSV_on_Blob_raw.

6. Click the drop-down to expand the options for Linked service and select + New.

For here, we are going to start defining the Linked service, which is a different Azure Data Factory resource that a Dataset is dependent on. We will continue this exercise in the next section.

Linked services

Linked services are objects that define the connection to the location where a data source resides. As mentioned earlier, the connection can be a type of database engine, a file share, a REST endpoint, or even a SaaS. Generally, the core information required is to define the location and provide credentials for authentication. Once a connection is successfully established, then it can be used as the transport layer to populate the datasets that are reliant on this connection. That is the role of a Linked service.

1. Picking up where we left off from the previous exercise, you should see the pane to establish a New linked service for Azure Blob Storage.

2. Give this linked service a name. For this exercise, we will name it Azure_Blob_LS.

3. Leave AutoResolveIntegrationRuntime selected as the Connect via integration runtime (IR). Integration runtime (IR) is an important component of ADF. IRs serve as proxy data gateways and are a software service that runs on non-domain controllers or on-premises servers. IRs are then used by ADF to connect to on-premises data sources. Acting as a proxy data gateway, organizations will not need to implement complex firewall exceptions for ADF to orchestrate on-premises data sources.

4. Leave Authentication method as Account key.

5. Next, remember the Azure Blob Storage we created earlier in this chapter? We will be using that storage location in this exercise. So, open a new tab or a different browser instance and go to https://portal.azure.com.

6. Navigate to the Azure Blob Storage resource we deployed earlier and copy the Storage account name and one of the Access keys.

7. Go back to Azure Data Factory.

8. Select Connection string, and select Enter manually as the option for Account selection method.

9. Copy and paste the Storage account name and Storage account key with information you retrieved from step 5.

Note   Technically, if Azure Data Factory and the Blob Storage are both in the same Azure subscription, as is the case in this exercise, we could have just selected From Azure subscription as the Account selection method and browse for the Azure Blob Storage instead of copying and pasting account names and keys. But, we did it this way in this exercise in order to demonstrate that the Azure Blob Storage may reside in a different subscription, and the only way to access that location is via other authentication methods. In this case, we used an access key, but we could also have used Azure Active Directory, Key Vault, or a temporary SAS key that is valid only for a period of time.

---

10. Click Test connection at the bottom of the pane and make sure the connection is successful. Then click Create.

11. We have now created a Linked service and are back to finalizing the details of the dataset. Click Browse, and select the bank.csv file located in the raw folder.

12. Check the box indicating First row as header.

13. Click Preview data to view a snapshot of the contents of the CSV file (a good way to quickly validate access). Close the preview window.

14. Click OK to complete the creation of the dataset.

Later in this chapter, we will create a Copy activity in the pipeline that would make use of the dataset.

Datasets and link services

In the last two exercises, we created a dataset and its underlying linked service in a single sequence because of their dependencies. If you browse Azure Data Factory now, you will see both objects exist in their respective locations in the editor. Because they are discrete objects, you can create a linked service object first and then use it in a dataset later. In fact, you can also reuse linked services. Now that we have a linked service to our Azure Blob Storage in Azure Data Factory, we do not have to recreate another linked service. If we need a different dataset populated with a different file from this same location, we will just reuse this linked service.

Cloning

Any resource in Azure Data Factory can be cloned. In this exercise, we will clone the CSV_on_Blob_raw dataset.

1. Click the ellipses next to CSV_on_Blob_raw dataset, and select Clone.

2. The dataset will be cloned with the same name and _copy1 appended. So, you should see CSV_on_Blob_raw_copy1 as a new dataset.

3. Rename this dataset CSV_on_Blob_stage.

4. Remove the contents, the container, directory, and filename. Enter stage as the File path, as seen in Figure 3-18. This dataset will be used as sink later in the chapter.

General   **Connection**   Schema   Parameters

| Linked service * | 🖼 Azure_Blob_LS ▼ | 🖋 Test connection | ✐ Open |

| File path * | stage | / | Directory | / | File |

| Compression type | none ▼ |

Figure 3-18. Editing the file path of a dataset

In this exercise, we explored the capability of cloning a resource like a dataset. In this modified dataset, we reused the linked service by not changing that field but pointed it to a different container in Azure Blob Storage.

You can also clone resources that contain other resources. For example, when you clone an entire pipeline that contains activities, the entire pipeline is cloned. Just be aware that the individual activities contained in the cloned pipeline are *not* cloned. So, if you modify the properties of an activity in the cloned pipeline, it is the *same* activity referenced by the original pipeline.

Next steps: Self-guided assignment

Before continuing, we will leave it up to you to go through the previous exercise once again to create another dataset for Azure SQL Database and its required linked service.

Important: If you do not have an Azure SQL Database already deployed or need instructions on deploying Azure SQL Database, please refer to this Microsoft quick start documentation to create an Azure SQL Database – https://docs.microsoft.com/en-us/azure/azure-sql/database/single-database-create-quickstart?tabs=azure-portal.

We will be using an Azure SQL Database for our hands-on exercises later in this chapter. **Please deploy an Azure SQL Database, and take note of the Server name, SQL Admin User Name, and Password (for use in our hands-on exercises later).**

Note   Use security best practices to access Azure SQL Databases and other Azure resources. To introduce concepts and promote the ease of going through the hands-on exercises, we will use default admin credentials and keys. These practices should not be used in a production environment.

Once you have created an Azure SQL Database, through the Azure portal, open the Azure SQL Database instance you created, and select Query editor from the right-hand side. Log in and paste the following query to create a table named bank, as shown in Figure 3-19. Click Run to execute the query.

```
CREATE TABLE bank (
    age int,
    job varchar(255),
    marital varchar(255),
    education varchar(255),
    Indefault varchar(255),
    balance float,
    housing varchar(10),
    loan varchar(10),
    deposit varchar(10)
);
```

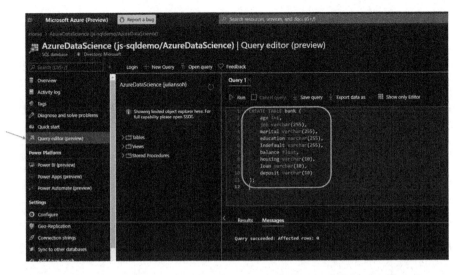

Figure 3-19. *Creating a table in an Azure SQL Database using Query editor in the Azure portal*

Hands-on: Creating a copy data pipeline

We are going to continue building pipeline1 that we created earlier in this chapter:

1. Select pipeline1.

2. On the editing canvas, note the location to define the properties associated to the pipeline vs. the location to define the properties of whichever activity is selected in the canvas, as depicted in Figure 3-20. Note that if you have multiple activities, the properties on the bottom will change depending on which activity you select in the canvas.

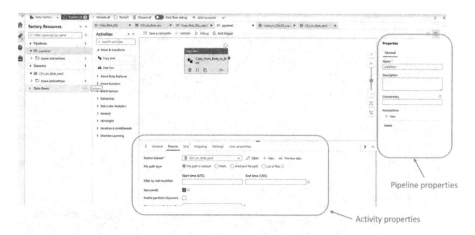

Figure 3-20. *Configuring properties for pipeline vs. activity*

3.   Rename pipeline1 to Copy_Blob_SQL.

4.   Select the Copy_from_Blob_to_Blob activity, and
      then click the Source tab in the properties below the
      canvas.

5.   Click the drop-down for Source dataset, and select
      CSV_on_Blob_raw as the dataset.

6.   Then click Open to open the dataset.

7.   Select the Connection tab, and make sure the box
      for First row as header is checked.

8.   Select the Schema tab, and if you do not see a
      schema, click Import schema and select from
      connection/store as the schema source. You should
      see the schema from the CSV file imported.

9. At the top of the canvas, select the Copy_Blob_SQL
    pipeline to view the entire pipeline.

10. Click the Sink tab in the properties pane beneath the
    canvas.

11. Select New next to the Sink dataset drop-down box.

12. Select the Azure tab, and pick Azure Blob Storage,
    and then click Continue.

13. Select DelimitedText as the format, and click
    Continue.

14. Type "CSV_on_Blob_stage" as the name of the
    dataset.

15. Click the drop-down list for Linked service, and
    select Azure_Blob_LS.

16. Click the folder icon in File path to browse the blob
    storage, and select stage. Then click OK.

17. Check the box for First row as header.

18. Click OK at the bottom of the pane.

19. Click back the pipeline. Then type .csv in the File
    extension box, as seen in Figure 3-21.

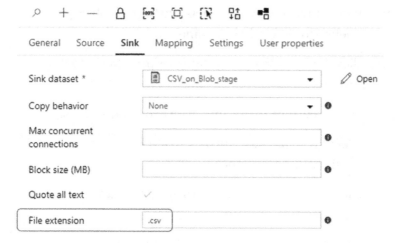

Figure 3-21. *Specifying the File extension*

20. Click Debug to run this pipeline.

21. The properties pane beneath the canvas will be focused on the Output tab. Click the icon that looks like a circled arrow to refresh and see the status of the pipeline, as seen in Figure 3-22.

Figure 3-22. *Status of pipeline execution*

22. The pipeline should have executed successfully. At this point, this pipeline has a single copy activity that copied a CSV file from one container in an Azure Blob Storage to another container in the same Azure Blob Storage. If we had used a different linked service for the sink dataset, this file would

have been moved to another Azure subscription, or
a completely different service altogether. Use Azure
Storage Explorer to verify that bank.csv was copied
into the container named "stage." You may need
to click the refresh icon at the top of the storage
explorer to see the new file.

Saving your work

Look at the top of the authoring workspace in Azure Data Factory, and you
will see a Publish all button with number next to it. This number tells you
the number of resources that have not been pushed to Azure Data Factory,
or a Git repo if source control was enabled.

Click Publish all and a separate pane will appear listing the pending
changes and new workloads that need to be published to Azure Data
Factory, as shown in Figure 3-23.

Publish all

You are about to publish all pending changes to the live environment. Learn more ☐

Pending changes (3)

NAME	CHANGE	EXISTING
◢ Pipelines		
⌗ Copy_Blob_SQL	(New)	-
◢ Datasets		
⌗ CSV_on_Blob_raw	(New)	-
⌗ CSV_on_Blob_stage	(New)	-

Figure 3-23. *Resources that need to be published to Azure Data
Factory*

Click the Publish button, and these resources will now be pushed up
to Azure Data Factory, GitHub, or Azure DevOps Repos depending on your
configuration.

Note   Publishing in Azure Data Factory is akin to saving your work. It is important to note that all changes remain in the browser session until it is published. Therefore, if you close the browser session without publishing your work, all the changes will be lost. During publishing, all changes will also be validated, and errors will have to be addressed before the work can be published. You can run a separate validation without publishing by clicking the Validate option located next to Debug.

Hands-on: Multiple activities in a pipeline

Usually, there are multiple activities in a pipeline. We can of course have one activity per pipeline and then have one pipeline trigger another pipeline, as shown in Figure 3-24, but that is not the best approach. The ability to execute another pipeline is useful when you are reusing exiting pipelines to build a new process, or for splitting up a pipeline that has too many activities and therefore difficult to keep track. We may also want to time the execution of a set of activities vs. a second set of activities so we can place them in two separate pipelines and trigger the execution of the second pipeline by the first pipeline if certain conditions are met.

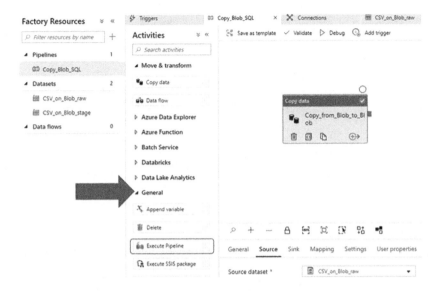

Figure 3-24. *Triggering the execution of another pipeline as one of the activities within a pipeline*

One easy strategy to adopt is to clone pipelines throughout the build stage so you can do unit testing as data is being copied and transformed from raw to stage.

In the preceding exercise, we now have a pipeline that copies data from one container to another (raw to stage) in Azure Blob Storage, and we know it works. In this exercise, we will continue building this pipeline by moving the data from the container name stage to the Azure SQL Database dataset you created earlier as part of your self-guided assignment.

1. Click the Copy_Blob_SQL pipeline.

2. Expand Move & transform, and drag a new Copy data activity and place it to the right of Copy_from_ Blob_to_Blob in the canvas, as seen in Figure 3-25.

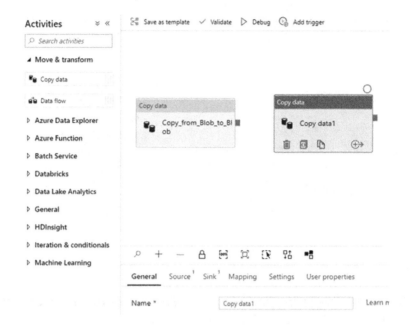

Figure 3-25. *New Copy data activity added to pipeline*

3. Rename the new Copy data activity from Copy data1
    to Copy_from_Blob_to_SQL.

4. Click the Source tab in the properties pane beneath
    the canvas, and select CSV_on_Blob_stage as the
    source dataset.

5. Click Preview data to see the data in the csv file. This
    also confirms that Azure Data Factory can access the
    file and can successfully read its contents. Close the
    preview pane when done.

6. Select Wildcard file path as the option for File path
    type.

7. In the Wildcard paths options, type *.csv in the
    Wildcard file name field, as shown in Figure 3-26.

| Wildcard paths | stage | / | Wildcard folder path | / | *.csv |

Figure 3-26. *Setting the suffix for wildcards*

8. Select the Sink tab, and click New to create a new sink dataset.

9. Select the Azure tab and pick Azure SQL Database. Then click Continue.

10. Name this dataset "bank_on_SQLDB."

11. Click the drop-down box for Linked service, and select New.

12. Name this new linked service "Azure_SQLDB_LS."

13. Select the Azure subscription where you had deployed the Azure SQL Database earlier in this chapter, and pick the server and database in the Server name and Database name fields, respectively.

14. Use SQL authentication type, and enter the sql admin username for the server and the password.

15. Click Test connection to ensure that your connection is successful.

16. Click Create.

17. Select the drop-down box in the Table name field, and select dbo.bank. You should have this table if you did the hands-on exercise earlier in this chapter (see Figure 3-19).

18. Click OK.

19. Back in the Copy_from_Blob_to_SQL Copy data activity, next to the Sink, click the Mapping tab, and then click Import schemas.

20. Azure Data Factory will attempt to map the fields between the source and sink datasets. Notice that it was not able to map one of the fields, as seen in Figure 3-27.

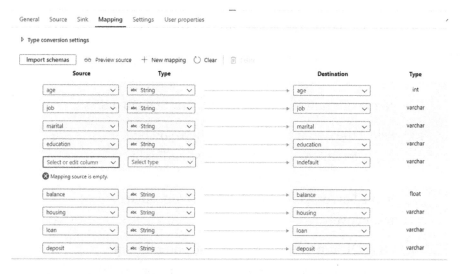

Figure 3-27. *Initial mapping of source and sink datasets*

21. Where the field names match up, ADF will map the fields accordingly. The field named "Indefault" in the sink does not have a matching source field, so we need to manually map the source field "default" to the sink field "Indefault" as shown in Figure 3-28.

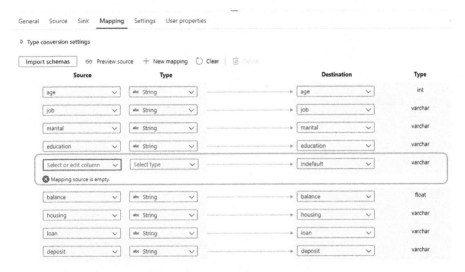

Figure 3-28. *Manually mapping fields*

22. Delete source fields that you do not need to copy into the Azure SQL Database by checking the field(s) and then clicking the trash can icon at the top of the mapping pane, as shown in Figure 3-29 (e.g., deleting loan and housing mapping).

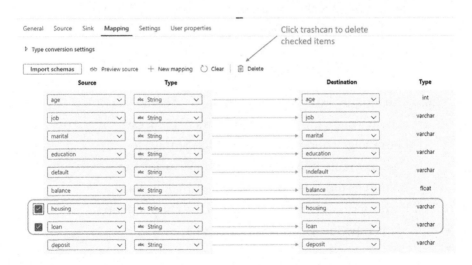

Figure 3-29. *Mapping and deleting fields between source and sink datasets*

23. Next, click and hold down the Success Output interface of the Copy_from_Blob_to_Blob activity and connect a line to the input interface of the Copy_from_Blob_to_SQL activity, as seen in Figure 3-30.

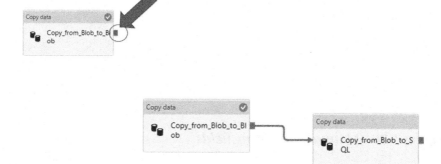

Figure 3-30. *Connecting two activities in a pipeline*

24. At the top of the canvas, click Debug.

25. The pipeline will now run in two stages. First, it will run the copy data activity to copy bank.csv from the raw container in Azure Blob Storage to the stage container in Azure Blob Storage.

26. The pipeline will then move to the next copy data activity where it will insert the rows in bank.csv in the stage container in Azure Blob Storage to the bank table in Azure SQL Database, using the mappings that were defined in step 10. Results of both successful stages are seen in the Output pane of the pipeline, as seen in Figure 3-31.

Figure 3-31. *Successful execution of a pipeline with multiple activities*

Validate that the data was successfully copied into Azure SQL Database by running a SELECT statement on table dbo.bank.

These exercises should have provided you with a basic foundation for how Azure Data Factory works. Although we only covered a very simple pipeline with only copy activities, you should explore the use of special activities that allow you to build logic into your pipelines, like the ForEach and DoUntil and If Condition loops located under Iteration & conditionals. Activities that do not have dependencies will execute in parallel.

More complex activities and the use of variables, parameters, and dynamically created content will be published on this book's GitHub repo located at `https://github.com/singh-soh`.

Accessing on-premises data sources

The existence of hybrid clouds will always exist; therefore, there is a need for a scenario where Azure Data Factory must connect to on-premises data sources to copy or move data to the cloud or vice versa.

This hybrid scenario is dependent on a special agent software called the self-hosted integration runtime (IR). The self-hosted integration runtime is an Azure Data Factory agent that runs on a computer that is connected to the on-premises environment, has access to the on-premises

data sources, and has outbound Internet connectivity to contact an Azure
Data Factory instance. In that sense, the self-hosted integration runtime
serves as a data gateway between the on-premises environment and Azure
Data Factory.

Architecture of the self-hosted integration runtime

Figure 3-32 from Microsoft's documentation is a great high-level depiction
of hybrid data flows involving the self-hosted integration runtime (source:
https://docs.microsoft.com/en-us/azure/data-factory/create-
self-hosted-integration-runtime).

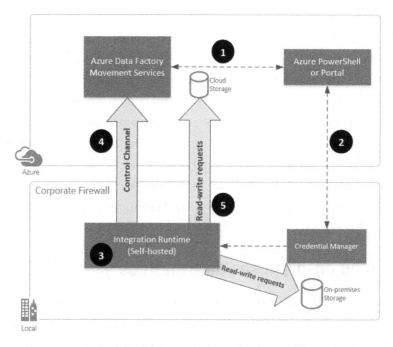

Figure 3-32. *High-level diagram of hybrid data flows using the self-
hosted IR (source – https://docs.microsoft.com/en-us/azure/
data-factory/create-self-hosted-integration-runtime)*

Installing and configuring the self-hosted integration runtime

Installing the self-hosted integration runtime is very extensively covered and very straightforward. You can find a forked copy of the latest instructions to install the self-hosted integration runtime at our GitHub repo located at `https://github.com/singh-soh/azure-docs/blob/master/articles/data-factory/create-self-hosted-integration-runtime.md`.

The installation and configuration of the self-hosted integration runtime is comprised of nine steps:

1. From the Azure portal, launch the authoring workspace in Azure Data Factory, and click Connections.

2. Click the Integration runtime tab, and click + New.

3. Select Azure, Self-Hosted, and then click Continue.

4. Select Self-Hosted, and then click Continue.

5. Provide a name for the self-hosted integration runtime, and then click Create.

6. Once created, you will be provided with two keys. Copy one set of keys that will be needed during the installation of the self-service integration runtime software later.

7. Identify a computer or virtual machine that will host the self-hosted integration runtime. There are special considerations, such as not hosting the self-hosted integration runtime together with a database server. Refer to the detailed documentation from our GitHub repo using the link at the top of this section.

8. Download the self-hosted integration runtime to the computer, and initiate the installation process.

9. When the installation is complete, it will ask for a key to register with an Azure Data Factory instance. Paste the key copied from step 6, and click Register.

That is basically the steps for deploying a self-hosted integration runtime. When you look in Azure Data Factory, you should be able to see the new self-hosted integration runtime and its status should be Running, as seen in Figure 3-33.

Figure 3-33. *Azure Data Factory showing the status of the self-hosted integration runtime*

Now, when you define datasets that are drawing from on-premises resources, you will need to define a Linked service that utilized the self-hosted integration runtime instead of the default AutoResolveIntegrationRuntime.

AutoResolveIntegrationRuntime is an Azure-based integration runtime used to connect to any Azure or Cloud-based endpoint. Self-hosted integration runtimes are used to access on-premises data sources or endpoints behind a firewall.

Summary

In this chapter, we explored the basics of *modern* data engineering and the tools that data engineers and data scientists should be familiar with, focusing primarily on Azure Data Factory as the data orchestration tool and Azure Blob Storage (or Data Lake Store) as the storage solution for datasets.

In Chapter 7, we will see how Azure Databricks can easily access Azure Blob and Data Lake Store to load datasets for transformation and analysis purposes. When we look at Azure Synapse, we will also see how Azure Synapse Analytics integrates with Azure Blob and Data Lake Store to load data using Polybase external tables.

Summary

CHAPTER 4

Introduction to Azure Machine Learning

In this chapter, we will study Azure ML platform and learn its capabilities, benefits, components, and advantages. In Chapter 5, we will do hands-on using Azure ML SDK and will understand how to build end-to-end machine learning solutions.

Machine learning primer

Machine learning (ML) at its most basic is a data science technique of using mathematical models of data to help a computer learn without being explicitly programmed to do so. It's considered a subset of artificial intelligence with statistics being at the heart. Machine learning algorithms can predict values, detect anomalies, determine structure, and create categories to identify patterns within data, and those patterns are then used to create a data model that can make predictions. But is it a new technology?

It was born from pattern recognition and the theory that computers can learn without being programmed to perform specific tasks. The next step was to create a set of instructions that would allow computers to learn from experience, that is, extract its own rules from large amount of data and use those rules for classification and prediction. The iterative aspect of machine learning is very important because as a model is exposed to

© Julian Soh and Priyanshi Singh 2020
J. Soh and P. Singh, *Data Science Solutions on Azure*,
https://doi.org/10.1007/978-1-4842-6405-8_4

unseen data, they are able to adapt independently. This was the beginning of machine learning and has led to the field that is collectively defined as artificial intelligence. It's a science that's not new – but one that has gained fresh momentum. So why now than ever?

While many machine learning algorithms have been around for a long time, the ability to automatically apply complex mathematical calculations to Big Data – over and over, faster and faster – is a recent development. Latest advancements in technology and resurgence interest in machine learning come from things like growing volume, velocity, variety and veracity of available data , computational processing that is cheaper and powerful, and storage that is more affordable and manageable due to cloud computing. Abundant and cheap computation has driven the abundance of data we are collecting and the increase in the capability of machine learning models. With all the demand in resources comes the demand of doing computational heavy machine learning processes in cloud. Machine learning coupled with cloud computing has been a game changing for business as it has resolved complex limitations of infrastructure and computation along with cost reduction.

Why machine learning on cloud?

Before we get to the overview of Azure Machine Learning (Azure ML), it is important to take the time to discuss benefits of machine learning on cloud. There are plenty of problems that cloud computing can solve pertaining to machine learning and artificial intelligence. From global corporations to small startup, non-profits, and government agencies, organizations at every level are benefitting from vast amount of resources, processing and supported infrastructure on cloud.

1. Easy to get started with no or little knowledge of machine learning and data science.

2. Cloud offers pay-as-you-go model to users for their heavy machine learning workloads allowing users to save infrastructure cost.

3. Availability of computational power ranging from CPUs, GPUs, FPGAs, and ASICs.

4. Scalable compute resources allow users to get started with machine learning experimentation on a smaller compute and scale up or scale out as it goes in production without changing code or environment.

5. Ability to change resources on the fly, use servers with predefined image and managed implementation of ML models.

6. Advanced skill set and artificial intelligence expertise are made accessible not only to data scientists but also developers and business users.

7. Flexibility to use open source frameworks like PyTorch, TensorFlow, CNTK, scikit-learn, MXNet, Chainer, and Keras with cloud resources.

Such capabilities are of great assistance in processing vast amount of data coming from multiple sources at a great speed. With cloud computing, users can spin up any number of servers, work on the algorithm, and destroy it after completion.

Microsoft Azure Machine Learning

Microsoft Azure Machine Learning (Azure ML) is a collection of services and tools that helps developers train, deploy, automate, manage, or track ML models in scalable cloud-based environment. It provides a range of cloud services including compute, storage, analytics, and networking. There are different ways to leverage this service, that is, use Python SDK/R SDK or zero code/low code option called Azure ML designer. The service supports thousands of open source packages available such as TensorFlow, PyTorch, CNTK, MXNet, Chainer, Keras, and scikit-learn. The supported ML tools make it easy and efficient to explore, transform, test, and deploy ML models, for example, Azure ML Visual Studio Code extension and Jupyter notebooks. Azure ML offers the following assets as part of the workspace:

1. Azure ML designer (low code/no code)

2. Azure ML Studio (classic)

3. Automated Machine Learning (AutoML – both UI and code)

4. Jupyter notebooks

5. RStudio

6. Datastore and Datasets

7. Compute instance

8. Compute targets/clusters

9. Inference clusters

10. Attached clusters

11. Experiments

12. Pipelines

13. Models

14. Endpoints

15. Data labeling

These assets are discussed in detail in this chapter, and we will do hands-on using these assets in Chapter 5. All these components provide users with following benefits:

1. Ingest data with no data limit from multiple Azure data sources

2. Scalable compute such as Azure Kubernetes Service (AKS) and Azure Databricks

3. Ease of pay-per-use cloud model depending on workloads

4. Ability to train models on your local machine and deploy on cloud

5. Integration with PowerBI to generate reports from deployed model

6. Supports data streaming process using Azure Event Hubs

7. Leverage Automated Machine Learning to find the most suited model

8. Supports pipelines to build iterative logical workflows and schedule them

9. Integration with Azure DevOps

10. Asynchronous predictions with real-time inferencing pipelines

Microsoft Azure ML service can be accessed through its Azure public cloud. Azure supports pre-built as well as custom machine learning development platforms, and depending on skills, users can leverage this platform to develop solutions. Typically, users can be put in the four categories of code or machine learning expertise.

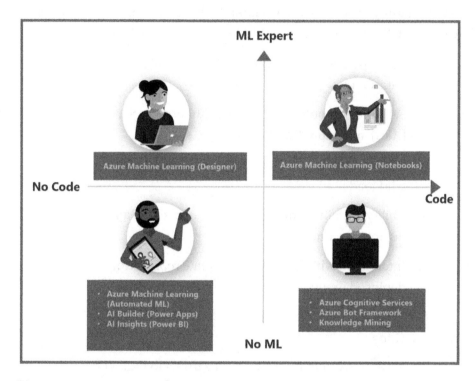

Figure 4-1. *Azure Machine Learning personas*

Azure ML service supports two editions – Basic and Enterprise. Once Basic edition is created, it can always be upgraded to Enterprise. The comparison of the supported features of both the editions can be found at `https://docs.microsoft.com/en-us/azure/machine-learning/concept-editions`.

The Azure ML workspace relies on a few Azure services: Azure Resource group, Azure Storage Account, Azure Application Insights, Azure Key Vault, and Azure Container Registry. These services get created automatically at the time of Azure ML service workspace creation; however, users are given flexibility to use preexisting services at the time of creating a new Azure ML workspace. Once Azure ML service workspace is created, launch the Azure ML Studio to access all the assets (discussed later in the chapter) supported in Azure ML as shown in Figure 4-2. Azure ML Studio is the web portal for data scientists and developers that supports Jupyter notebook servers, Azure ML designer (in preview at the time of writing this book), and Automated Machine Learning (AutoML – also in preview at the time of writing this book).

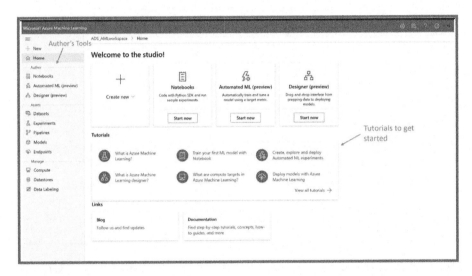

Figure 4-2.   *Azure ML service workspace*

This is the latest release of Azure ML which includes Python/R SDK and the drag-and-drop designer to build and deploy machine learning models. There is an initial implementation of Machine Learning Studio as well which is now called the Azure ML Studio (classic) which offers standalone drag-and-drop experience of pre-built machine learning algorithms along with Python/R drag-and-drop execute actions. Figure 4-3 summarizes the differences between two offerings. Please refer to this repo `https://github.com/singh-soh/AzureDataScience/tree/master/Chapter04_AzureML_Part1` to learn how to create the workspace.

Feature	Machine Learning Studio (classic)	Azure Machine Learning
Drag and drop interface	Supported	Supported - Azure Machine Learning designer (preview) (Requires Enterprise workspace)
Experiment	Scalable (10-GB training data limit)	Scale with compute target
Training compute targets	Proprietary compute target, CPU support only	Wide range of customizable training compute targets. Includes GPU and CPU support
Deployment compute targets	Proprietary web service format, not customizable	Wide range of customizable deployment compute targets. Includes GPU and CPU support
ML Pipeline	Not supported	Build flexible, modular pipelines to automate workflows
MLOps	Basic model management and deployment	Entity versioning (model, data, workflows), workflow automation, integration with CICD tooling, and more
Model format	Proprietary format, Studio (classic) only	Multiple supported formats depending on training job type
Automated model training and hyperparameter tuning	Not supported	Supported in the SDK and visual workspace
Data drift detection	Not supported	Supported in SDK and visual workspace

Figure 4-3. *Comparing Azure ML Studio (classic) and Azure ML. Source: `https://docs.microsoft.com/en-us/azure/machine-learning/compare-azure-ml-to-studio-classic`*

Azure Machine Learning workspace

Azure ML workspace is a top-level resource providing a central place to access and work with all the artifacts or components to manage every aspect of AI and machine learning aspect. Azure ML workspace is comprised of visual drag-and-drop designer, Azure ML SDK, Automated ML (AutoML), and the tools used to implement historical runs, model versions, track metrics, deployments, logs, and so on. It supports RBAC – role-based access control – to define access within team members as well. The workspace can also be tied up to Azure DevOps repos to implement CI/CD pipelines and fully automate the process via MLOps. Figure 4-4 shows the Azure ML taxonomy to understand Azure ML components.

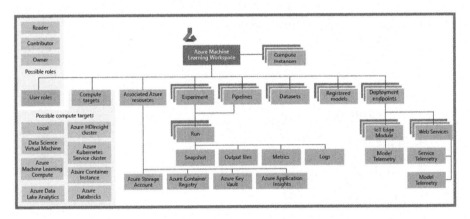

Figure 4-4. *Azure ML component. Source:* `https://docs.microsoft.com/en-us/azure/machine-learning/concept-workspace`

Azure Machine Learning workflow

Azure ML provides tools to execute repeatable ML workflow of data preparation, transformation, training, tuning, evaluation, deployment, and inference. The service user interface allows you to navigate through the workflow implemented via code or visual designer. The workflow is shown in Figure 4-5.

125

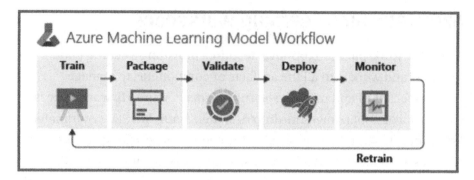

Figure 4-5. *Azure ML workflow. Source:* `https://docs.microsoft.`
`com/en-us/azure/machine-learning/concept-azure-machine-`
`learning-architecture`

To achieve the preceding workflow, Azure ML service workspace can
be broken down into the following elements:

1. Datastores and Datasets

2. Compute

3. Experiment

4. Pipelines

5. Models

6. Endpoints

From training the model to packaging, validating, deploying, and
monitoring, there are interactions involved at each stage, and with the
given set of Azure ML tools, the user can navigate back and forth smoothly
and track the workflow. Each stage in the workflow can also demand a
dedicated fleet of servers or memory to accelerate the processing. For
example, Apache Spark clusters are commonly used in data preparation
of a large dataset, a GPU-enabled virtual machine is ideal to train the
model or to tune the hyperparameters and a different compute can
be used for scoring the model, and ultimately, a Kubernetes cluster is

leveraged to run containerized model for inference. Whether the workflow run on developer workstation or run on a cluster of VMs on cloud, these dependencies are common and Azure ML serves these functionalities via the previously mentioned assets.

In the next section, we will discuss how to achieve the workflow with Azure ML tools.

Azure Machine Learning Datastores and Datasets

Datastores and Datasets are the reference points to the data sources and are attached to the workspace. Datastores can store connection information to Azure data sources so they can be referred to by the name and not have to use connection information, access keys, secrets, or authentication information to connect to the data sources. For example, organizations can create datastores to give data access to a team of data scientists by sharing datastore name rather than sharing data source credentials. It provides a layer of abstraction over Azure data sources. Azure ML supports the following services that can be registered as Datastores:

1. Azure Blob Storage

2. Azure File Share

3. Azure Data Lake Storage Gen1 and Gen2

4. Azure SQL Database

5. Azure Database for PostgreSQL

6. Databricks File System

7. Azure Database for MySQL

Each workspace has default Datastores, that is, the Azure Blob Storage and Azure File Share from the Azure Storage Account that gets created automatically with the service. Users can register additional Datastores from the portal or from the code. This chapter covers UI experience of Azure ML. The next chapter covers hands-on with Azure ML. Figure 4-6 shows creating datastore from the portal.

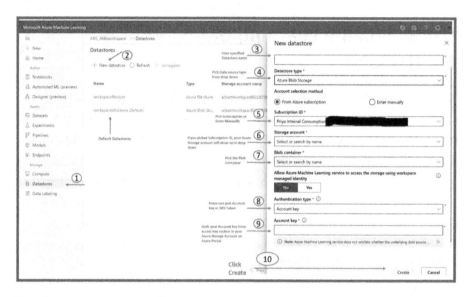

Figure 4-6. *Azure ML Datastore creation*

One level down comes the Datasets. The Dataset is the reference to data location in Datastores along with a copy of its metadata or public web URLs. Users can create datasets and reference files/tables in Azure data sources; as data remains in existing data source, there is no additional storage cost. For example, a table will be a dataset in Azure SQL Database referenced as Datastore. Datasets support two types: Tabular Dataset and File Dataset that allow users to consume raw data, transform, manage, and perform actions on data. Datasets can be used in Azure ML pipelines as well; we will cover that in later section. Tabular Dataset allows users to access tabular format by parsing file or list of files into pandas or spark dataframe. Users can create TabularDataset object from .csv, tsv, parquet, .json, and from SQL query results. On the other hand, File Dataset allows you to download or mount the single or multiple files of any format to your compute as FileDataset object enabling users to work on wider range of data format in machine learning or deep learning scenarios.

Apart from public URLs, Azure ML also offers ML-ready curated data from open domains that allows users to access open data in experiments from a common storage location without creating a copy of data in your storage account. Open domain datasets, for example, public holidays, NOAA weather, US population, and multiple-city safety data, are stored in parquet format in East US Azure region. Users don't need Azure account to access open datasets; they can be accessed using code or Azure service interface or Python/Spark environment. Figure 4-7 demonstrates how users can create datasets from the portal.

Figure 4-7. *Azure ML Dataset creation*

Azure Machine Learning compute and development environments

Compute lets you specify where you run your training script and host your service deployment ranging from your local machine to cloud-based compute resource. Azure ML supports multiple types of computes for experimentation, training, production, and for inferencing under pay-per-use cloud model allowing users to implement a flexible data science ecosystem. For example, code can be developed and tested on local or low-cost compute and then moved to more scalable compute such as spark clusters for production workloads. Individual processes can be run on required compute configuration at different stages and times, and that's the key benefit of cloud computing. For example, users can leverage GPU-based compute to train on large datasets and switch to lighter/lower cost CPU model for testing/scoring purposes. Users can take advantage of this principle by defining compute targets that can scale as well as start/stop automatically based on workload processing needs. Azure ML is platform agnostic, and it's important to understand the benefits of different development environments to work with Azure ML. As compute can be picked by the user, let's talk about development environments users can get started with. Figure 4-8 summarizes the pros and cons of different development environments.

Environment	Pros	Cons
Cloud-based Azure Machine Learning compute instance (preview)	Easiest way to get started. The entire SDK is already installed in your workspace VM, and notebook tutorials are pre-cloned and ready to run.	Lack of control over your development environment and dependencies. Additional cost incurred for Linux VM (VM can be stopped when not in use to avoid charges). See pricing details.
Local environment	Full control of your development environment and dependencies. Run with any build tool, environment, or IDE of your choice.	Takes longer to get started. Necessary SDK packages must be installed, and an environment must also be installed if you don't already have one.
Azure Databricks	Ideal for running large-scale intensive machine learning workflows on the scalable Apache Spark platform.	Overkill for experimental machine learning, or smaller-scale experiments and workflows. Additional cost incurred for Azure Databricks. See pricing details.
The Data Science Virtual Machine (DSVM)	Similar to the cloud-based compute instance (Python and the SDK are pre-installed), but with additional popular data science and machine learning tools pre-installed. Easy to scale and combine with other custom tools and workflows.	A slower getting started experience compared to the cloud-based compute instance.

Figure 4-8. *Development environments comparison. Source:* `https://docs.microsoft.com/en-us/azure/machine-learning/` `how-to-configure-environment`

In this chapter, we will do hands-on using cloud-based Azure ML compute instance. Please follow the sources in Figure 4-8 if you're using other development environments.

Azure Machine Learning compute instance

Azure ML compute instance is a cloud-based virtual machine that serves as development environment for data scientists. It's integrated with Azure ML workspace and studio where users can share Jupyter notebooks and data with other data scientists. It gives one click setup to launch JupyterLab, Jupyter, and RStudio with pre-configured ML packages like TensorFlow, PyTorch, Azure ML libraries, deep learning, and GPU drivers. Users can launch their preferred Python/R language tools and build models using integrated notebooks and also customize by installing packages via terminals and drivers for advanced scenarios. SSH into compute instance is disabled by default but can be enabled at compute instance creation time allowing users to leverage public/private key mechanism. Compute instance can also be used as training compute targets from your local environment or local inferencing deployment target for testing/debugging purposes. Compute instance can be created from the portal, integrated notebook experience, Azure ML SDK, and Azure CLI. Figure 4-9 shows how to create compute instance from the portal.

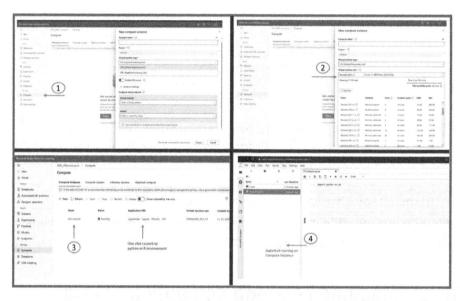

Figure 4-9. *Azure ML compute instance and JupyterLab creation*

The underlying default storage account serves as the common storage for all the Jupyter notebooks, files, and R scripts created from all the compute instances in the same workspace and hence makes it easy to share code among team members. Azure File Share account of the workspace is mounted as a drive on compute instance, and all the code lives under "User files" directory, so when a user stops or deletes the compute instance, the notebooks or scripts are safely preserved. The user may want to create temporary files in development process; they can create a directory /tmp for temporary data which will not be accessible to other compute instances. For R users, Azure ML offers RStudio on compute instance or R SDK (in public preview currently) via IDE or notebooks. Figure 4-10 shows how RStudio browser looks on compute instance on Azure portal.

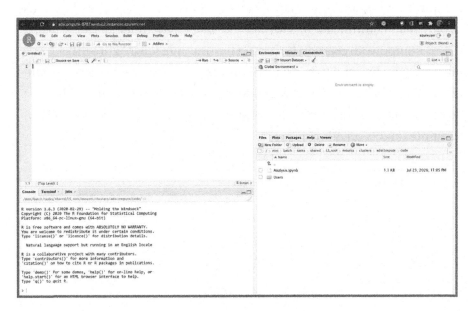

Figure 4-10. *Azure ML compute instance RStudio*

Azure Machine Learning compute target

Compute target is a resource that provides virtual components by combining CPUs/GPUs, memory, and disks to create a virtual machine. This resource could be a local machine or a cloud-based environment. The idea is to provide virtual or physical servers and storage devices that are comprised of high availability, automatic scalability, and on-demand consumption and shared by multiple users. Azure ML supports a variety of compute targets/resources to run scripts to train, test, validate models, and host your service deployment. Compute targets other than the local machine can be shared among multiple users in a workspace and are given flexibility to configure compute based on the requirement in model development life cycle. For example, users can develop and test on small amount of data using local environment or cloud-based VM as dev and compute environment, scale to larger data or distributed training by using compute targets, and, once satisfactory model is ready to be deployed, use deployment compute targets for web hosting environment.

As compute targets can be reused for multiple jobs, Azure ML pipelines can be used to build pipeline steps execution for each compute target. We will discuss Azure ML pipelines later in this chapter and will do hands-on in the next chapter. Figure 4-11 summarizes the available compute targets on Azure.

Training targets	Automated ML	ML pipelines	Azure Machine Learning designer
Local computer	yes		
Azure Machine Learning compute cluster	yes & hyperparameter tuning	yes	yes
Azure Machine Learning compute instance	yes & hyperparameter tuning	yes	
Remote VM	yes & hyperparameter tuning	yes	
Azure Databricks	yes (SDK local mode only)	yes	
Azure Data Lake Analytics		yes	
Azure HDInsight		yes	
Azure Batch		yes	

Figure 4-11. *Azure ML compute targets for model training. Source:* `https://docs.microsoft.com/en-us/azure/machine-learning/concept-compute-target`

Azure ML compute clusters are single- or multi-node clusters of virtual machines that automatically scale up and down based on the workload. This is one of the key objectives to use compute targets to run training jobs as it's cost effective to run experiments on large volumes of data and use parallel processing to distribute the workload. Azure ML compute cluster (refer to Figure 4-12) autoscales to zero or user-defined minimum node when idle; however, compute instance doesn't. Users should stop the compute instance after use to avoid unnecessary cost.

Note   Azure ML compute instance and compute clusters are the only managed computes in Azure ML; however, users can create a compute target outside of Azure ML and attach it to the workspace, for example, Azure Databricks cluster.

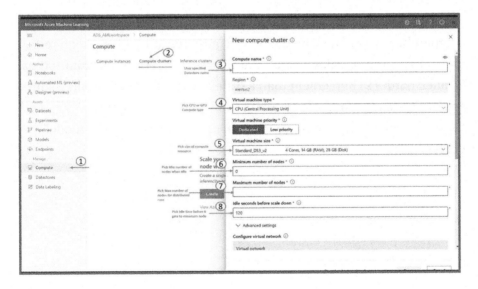

Figure 4-12. *Azure ML compute clusters*

Azure Machine Learning inference clusters

Inference clusters are the resources used to host the web service containing your model. This is typically the last step in model development life cycle after the user is satisfied with the model's performance and has validated the model and debugged any errors. There could be two types of inference – batch inference and real-time inference – and for each type, different clusters are recommended to meet the requirement. Batch inferencing is a process of generating predictions on a batch of observations on a recurring schedule (e.g., hourly, weekly). For such inferencing, latency is typically on the orders of hours or days, and users can also leverage spark support for Big Data. Azure ML compute clusters are a good choice for batch inferencing. On the other hand, real-time inferencing is the process of generating predictions in real time upon request and also referred to as dynamic inferencing. These predictions are generated on a single observation of data at runtime without having to wait for hours/days for batch predictions. This type of inferencing is more complex because of the added tooling, compute, and a system required for latency – a system that needs to respond with prediction within 100ms is much harder to implement than a system with a SLA of 24 hours. Azure supports different compute targets to meet inferencing requirements, and Figure 4-13 shows a great comparison of different resources for model deployment.

Compute target	Used for	GPU support	FPGA support	Description
Local web service	Testing/debugging			Use for limited testing and troubleshooting. Hardware acceleration depends on use of libraries in the local system.
Azure Machine Learning compute instance web service	Testing/debugging			Use for limited testing and troubleshooting.
Azure Kubernetes Service (AKS)	Real-time inference	Yes (web service deployment)	Yes	Use for high-scale production deployments. Provides fast response time and autoscaling of the deployed service. Cluster autoscaling isn't supported through the Azure Machine Learning SDK. To change the nodes in the AKS cluster, use the UI for your AKS cluster in the Azure portal. AKS is the only option available for the designer.
Azure Container Instances	Testing or development			Use for low-scale CPU-based workloads that require less than 48 GB of RAM.
Azure Machine Learning compute clusters	Batch inference	Yes (machine learning pipeline)		Run batch scoring on serverless compute. Supports normal and low-priority VMs.
Azure Functions	(Preview) Real-time inference			
Azure IoT Edge	(Preview) IoT module			Deploy and serve ML models on IoT devices.
Azure Data Box Edge	Via IoT Edge		Yes	Deploy and serve ML models on IoT devices.

Figure 4-13. *Azure ML compute targets for model deployment. Source:* `https://docs.microsoft.com/en-us/azure/machine-learning/concept-compute-target`

The usual model deployment includes three components:

1. Inference environment: This environment is defined to capture the software dependencies required to run your model for inference. For example, it can include Python version or libraries required to run the script.

2. Scoring script or entry script: This script is the engine of your inferencing job. It receives the data submitted to a deployed web service, retrieves the ML model from AZUREML_MODEL_DIR, and

137

passes the data to the model. The script is unique to your model and should understand what the data model expects and results that model returns.

3. Inference configuration: This encapsulates inference environment, software dependencies, scoring script, Python version, and workspace required for your model to run as a web service.

We will learn how to create environments, scoring script, and inference configurations to learn about deploying your model as a web service in Chapter 5. Inference cluster can be created in similar manner as Azure ML compute clusters in Azure ML workspace.

Azure Machine Learning attached compute

Attached compute also referred as unmanaged compute is the compute not managed by Azure ML. This compute is created outside of Azure ML such as Databricks cluster, virtual machine, Data Lake Analytics, or HDInsight and attached to the Azure ML workspace. Figure 4-14 shows how you can attach the compute in Azure ML workspace.

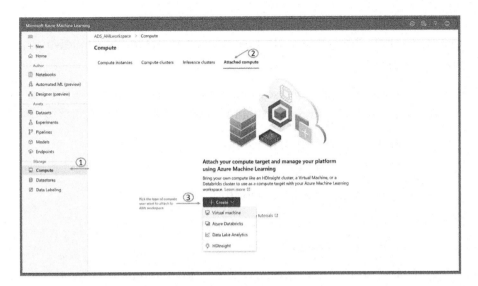

Figure 4-14. *Azure ML attached compute*

Azure Machine Learning experiments

Machine learning model development includes many steps from architecting the model to finally yielding the results; often these steps are iterative, and it's important to keep track of metrics, model versions, hyperparameter combinations, and compute target to recreate the environment and maintain the complex flow of the process. To support iterative experimentation and tracking log metrics, Azure ML offers a simple-to-use Python API to provide a seamless machine learning experimentation process. An Experiment class is a container of trials or runs to construct a predictive analysis model. An experiment is represented by Experiment class, trials are represented by Run class, and run configurations are represented by Estimator class. Estimators are used to create an environment/configuration for training scripts leveraging learning frameworks like scikit-learn, PyTorch, and TensorFlow. Azure ML supports creating the different types of experiments such as Automated

ML experiment (AutoML) and creating pipelines using designer (drag and drop), via Python code or UI. An experiment includes the following characteristics:

1. Dataset: Data to be used in modeling process for machine learning experimentation.

2. Module or algorithm or estimator: An algorithm or set of algorithms (AutoML).

3. Input/output ports for algorithms data flow.

4. Parameters (optional): Algorithms depending on parameters should be set.

Figure 4-15 shows how you can create an experiment in Azure ML workspace UI.

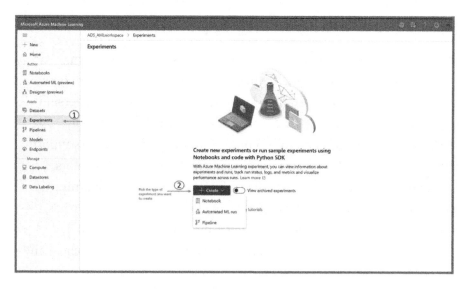

Figure 4-15. *Azure ML experiments*

Before we discuss how to create an experiment, it's important to know the types of experiments the user can create. This chapter will demonstrate creating experiments using Azure ML workspace UI; we will cover end-to-end machine learning development using Azure ML SDK in notebooks in Chapter 5.

Azure Machine Learning pipelines

Machine learning workflows involve complex step-by-step process of data preparation, transformation, feature engineering, training, tuning, deployment, and inference. A single notebook running all of these steps can really hamper the performance and may run out of resources while dealing with larger datasets or distributed operations in the workflow. The idea behind introducing pipelines is to manage end-to-end workflows by providing different set of hardware and software requirements and environment for each step, hence making each step unique and independent of each other. For example, for larger datasets, data preparation step may require CPUs or spark clusters, while training and tuning of machine learning models may require GPUs; with pipelines, the user can configure these requirements for individual step. Azure ML Pipelines optimize the workflows by providing distinct toolkit and frameworks for each step making users focus more on building solutions rather than infrastructure. Once the pipeline is designed, often data sources change, or there is more fine-tuning requirement around training. When pipeline is rerun, the execution jumps to the step which needs to rerun and skips what hasn't changed like unchanged training scripts or metadata which makes the machine learning workflows optimized. This capability not only speeds up the execution but also saves the compute resources and hence the cost.

With Azure ML pipelines, the dependencies between steps are orchestrated automatically. The orchestration between steps might include spinning up and down docker images, attaching and detaching compute resources, and intermediate data sharing with downstream compute targets automatically. Azure ML pipelines provide a collaborative environment for data scientists and data engineers to build pipeline steps concurrently by allowing team members to track a version of data sources, inputs, and outputs instead of manually tracking iterations with data and results. Users can stay on top of changing data by scheduling pipelines or configuring them to be event driven.

Pipelines integrate with all the Azure ML assets such as experiments, datasets, compute, models, and endpoints. While pipelines are used for data preparation, transformation, and training of models, one of the primary use cases for pipelines is batch inferencing. After building the pipeline, users can publish it and configure a REST endpoint that can be triggered from any HTTP library in any language on any platform. Azure ML leverages *Pipeline* object to perform all the operations, and Figure 4-16 shows the high-level flow of actions in Azure ML workspace.

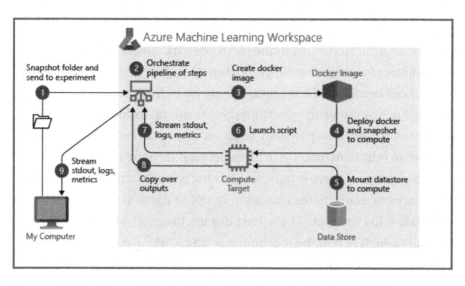

Figure 4-16. *Azure ML pipelines flow. Source:* `https://docs.microsoft.com/en-us/azure/machine-learning/concept-ml-pipelines`

Azure ML uses *PipelineStep* as the base class which contains actual steps as subclasses such as *EstimatorStep, PythonScriptStep, DataTransferStep, ParallelRunStep, or ModuleStep. PythonScriptStep* is the most flexible subclass as it can be customized to any requirement. *ParallelRunStep* can be used to process large amounts of data asynchronously and in parallel. *ModuleStep* holds reusable computation such as scripts and executables which can be shared among pipelines and multiple users. Other subclasses like *DataTransferStep* can help achieve the functionality with less code. For example, *DataTransferStep* can be created by just passing the name of step and compute targets with input and output locations. For each step, *Pipeline* object collects compute resources, OS resources (docker images), software resources (conda/virtualenv dependencies), and data inputs.

Azure ML pipelines can be built either through Python SDK or the Azure ML designer available in enterprise edition. The Python SDK provides more control and flexibility over customization, and we will cover hands-on on SDK in Chapter 5.

Azure Machine Learning designer pipelines

Azure ML designer is the newly released version of Azure ML Studio (classic). As discussed earlier in the chapter, Azure ML designer provides drag-and-drop visual interface experience of building experiments with auto scalable Azure ML compute clusters at each module. This is one of the key differentiators in the classic Azure ML Studio and the new Azure ML designer. With autoscaling, users can now start with smaller models or data without worrying about expanding to production workloads with bigger data or heavier models. Another key benefit of new designer is the ease of deployment. Users can now deploy their trained models without getting into the heavy coding, container services, or docker/Kubernetes environment and model management. Azure ML designer provides deployment of model with batch inferencing or real-time inferencing with a few clicks after the user has tuned the model with several experiments and is satisfied with model's performance. Once the model is deployed, users can test the web service immediately with pre-populated input data within the designer. This saves a lot of time for users to have a fully functioning web service. Lastly, Azure ML designer integrates completely with Azure ML service SDK experiments, compute, models, images, and deployment. This allows users to have the best of both worlds – drag and drop and code based with inherited capabilities like run history, logged metrics, and versioning. An Azure ML designer pipeline which runs as an experiment once the user submits it is shown in Figure 4-17.

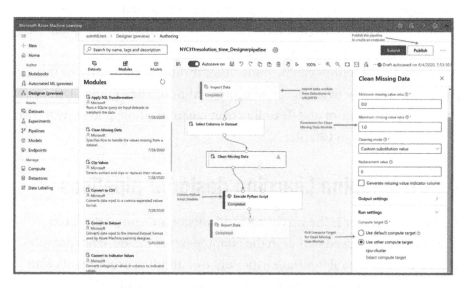

Figure 4-17. *Azure ML designer overview*

Azure ML designer is completely web based with no software installation required. An experiment in Azure ML designer is comprised of Datastores, modules, pipelines, Datasets, compute targets, registered models (discussed later in the chapter), and published batch or real-time inference endpoints. A module in designer can be considered as any algorithm or data ingestion or data preparation/transformation functions. Azure ML designer pipelines are built by dragging the datasets and existing or custom language modules and dropping them to connect with right data flow. Existing modules include everything from data ingestion to data transformation to model selection to deployment and scoring.

Custom language modules include bringing your own custom Python or R scripts to include additional functionality or models in the experiment, giving users the flexibility to use only existing or custom or a combination of both the modules. Users are also prompted with parameters when they select the module to help tune the model.

Azure ML designer pipelines can be any course of action such as prediction in real time or in batch or a pipeline to just transform data-allowing users to reuse the work and collaborate with low-code, no-code approach. We will develop a solution on real use case using Azure ML designer as well as Azure ML SDK in Chapter 5. The following is a flow diagram to understand designer pipeline execution in multiple scenarios (Figure 4-18).

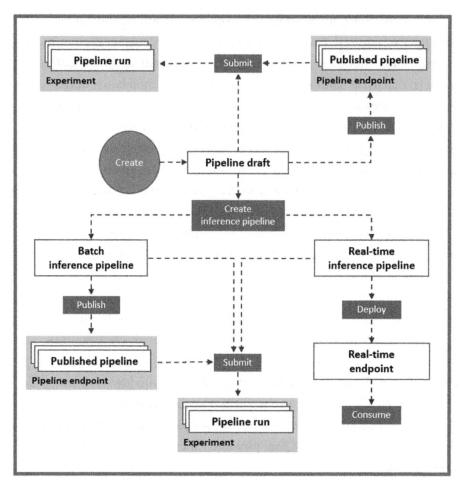

Figure 4-18. *Azure ML designer pipeline execution. Source:* `https://docs.microsoft.com/en-us/azure/machine-learning/concept-designer`

Azure Machine Learning models and endpoints

Model class is defined as packaging of the model to provide a location and the version. A model can be the result of Azure ML run or Automated ML (AutoML) run or some other model trained outside of Azure. Users can bring their locally trained models to this class and register them in the workspace. Usually multiple experiment runs would yield different models; the idea to use this class is to profile some of those models that contribute to good performance. Registering a model creates a logical container for the files that make up your model along with model metadata like model description, tags, and framework information. The profiled or registered model can then be used to understand deployment requirements and use it with docker or can be deployed to an inference endpoint as a web service. Figure 4-19 shows how the user can bring the model trained outside Azure to Azure ML workspace and register it.

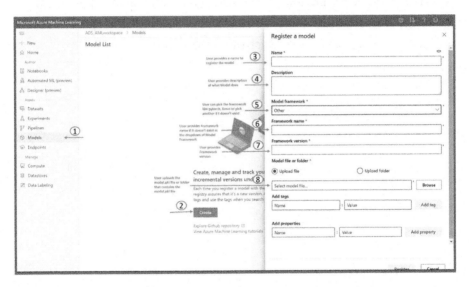

Figure 4-19. *Azure ML models registration*

Endpoints represent the Azure ML object that takes features as inputs, applies a specified machine learning model, and returns the output. Azure ML model deployed as web service creates a REST API endpoint. In Azure ML, pipelines can also be deployed for batch or real-time inference and exist as a web service. These endpoints can then be plugged as REST API in any application, dashboard, or other Azure services.

Summary

In this chapter, we covered the important topic of the rise of machine learning on cloud and learned Azure ML assets to build, train, tune, deploy, and track machine learning models. We looked at the Azure ML workspace user interface and no code ways of leveraging the data science tools. All these topics are covered in greater detail in Chapter 5 with hands-on experience to leverage Azure ML SDK. Additional documentation and videos for this chapter are shared on GitHub repo at `https://github.com/singh-soh/AzureDataScience/tree/master/Chapter04_AzureML_Part1`, and documentation on Azure ML can be found at `https://docs.microsoft.com/en-us/azure/machine-learning/`.

CHAPTER 5

Hands-on with Azure Machine Learning

In the previous chapter, we discussed Azure Machine Learning service tools, functionality, and assets. This chapter focuses on providing hands-on experience to users and develop end-to-end machine learning project life cycle using Azure ML SDK. As mentioned in the previous chapter, Azure ML offers Python SDK, R SDK, and low-code or zero-code Azure ML designer approaches to develop, train, and deploy ML models; we will use Python SDK for our hands-on labs in this chapter. For the purposes of hands-on lab in this chapter, we will assume users are familiar with Python and getting started with implementing data science solutions on cloud.

Lab setup

Let's get started with setting up the lab environment! To follow the hands-on lab in this chapter, users need to have an Azure subscription. Users can also sign up for a free Azure subscription worth $200 here (`https://azure.microsoft.com/en-us/free/`). After signing up, users will be able to create Azure ML service from the portal (`https://portal.azure.com/`) or Azure gov portal (`https://portal.azure.us`).

© Julian Soh and Priyanshi Singh 2020
J. Soh and P. Singh, *Data Science Solutions on Azure*,
https://doi.org/10.1007/978-1-4842-6405-8_5

> **Note**   Azure ML is currently available in two Azure Government
> regions: US Gov Arizona and US Gov Virginia with basic edition being
> generally available and enterprise edition in preview. The service in
> Azure Government is in feature parity with Azure commercial cloud.
> Refer to this link for more info: `https://azure.microsoft.com/`
> `en-us/updates/azure-machine-learning-available-in-`
> `us-gov/`.

For hands-on lab in this chapter, we will use the following resources:

- Bank marketing dataset posted here (`https://github.`
  `com/singh-soh/AzureDataScience/tree/master/`
  `datasets/Bank%20Marketing%20Dataset`). Original
  source `www.kaggle.com/janiobachmann/bank-`
  `marketing-dataset`.

- Compute instance as development environment (note:
  as explained in the previous chapter, users can also
  use local computer, DSVM, or Databricks). Azure ML
  SDK needs to be installed when working on local or in
  Databricks; please follow the instructions here to set up
  in your local environment/Databricks:

  `https://docs.microsoft.com/en-us/azure/`
  `machine-learning/how-to-configure-`
  `environment`

- JupyterLab notebooks (already installed on compute
  instance).

Note   Azure ML extension is also available if you prefer visual studio code. The extension supports Python features as well as Azure ML functionalities to make the development environment handier. Refer here to install the extension:

```
https://marketplace.visualstudio.com/
items?itemName=ms-toolsai.vscode-ai
```

To create the Azure ML workspace, go to Azure portal and follow these steps:

1. From the Azure portal, type "Machine Learning" (without quotes) in the search box at the top of the page.

2. Click Machine Learning in the search results.

3. Click + Add.

4. Create a new resource group or select an existing one.

5. Provide a name for the Azure ML workspace.

6. For location, select a region closest to you.

7. For workspace edition, select Enterprise edition. We will use Enterprise edition for the hands-on lab. Building AutoML experiments on Azure ML Studio is not supported in basic edition. Please refer to here to see capabilities in basic and enterprise edition:

    ```
    https://docs.microsoft.com/en-us/azure/
    machine-learning/concept-editions
    ```

8. Click Review + Create, and then click Create in the subsequent screen.

The workspace will take few minutes to get deployed; grab a coffee meanwhile. Once the workspace is created, users will see the service on the portal shown in Figure 5-1.

Figure 5-1. *Azure ML workspace on Azure PortalClick on "Launch now" to launch the workspace. Once the workspace is launched, you will see the workspace as shown in Figure 5-2*

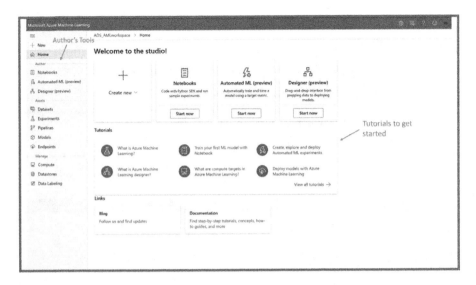

Figure 5-2. *Azure ML Studio workspace*

In the previous chapter, we covered all the assets and concepts of Azure ML workspace. In this chapter, we will use those assets to build our analysis on bank marketing dataset.

Getting started with JupyterLab

JupyterLab is the latest integration of Jupyter notebooks with activities like text editors, terminals, and custom components like code console in a flexible, extensible, and more IDE-like experience. For beginner, Jupyter notebook is a great start, and as you become more familiar and want to have more features, switch to JupyterLab. To get started with your JupyterLab, follow these steps:

1. Click Compute.

2. Under Compute Instance, create a new compute instance without any advanced settings (explained in Chapter 4, Figure 4-9).

153

3. Once compute instance is created, click JupyterLab
    to launch it.

4. Under Users, click your name and create a folder
    called "BankMarketingAnalysis."

5. Under "BankMarketingAnalysis Folder," create a
    Python 3.6 Azure ML notebook.

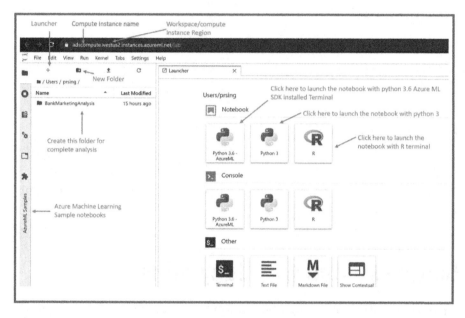

Figure 5-3. *Azure ML compute instance JupyterLab*

Note   If you create simple Python 3 notebook, you will need to
install Azure ML SDK by going to terminal to be able to use it in
notebook. The terminal can be changed after creating the notebook
as well.

Prerequisite setup

Now that we are in JupyterLab on compute instance, let's start writing code to build the model. The following steps are logistics/setup for Azure ML training:

- Create a Jupyter notebook.

- Initialize Azure ML workspace.

- Create an Experiment.

- Create Azure ML compute cluster.

- Default/register new Datastores.

- Upload data to datastores.

To get started, follow these steps:

1. Create a Jupyter notebook, and put the following code. To follow along with the code, users can also Git clone the repository from GitHub. To do that, refer to the following location. We will be using BankMarketingTrain.ipynb notebook for the code.

   ```
   https://github.com/singh-soh/
   AzureDataScience/tree/master/Chapter05_
   AzureML_Part2
   ```

2. Initialize the Azure ML workspace. Run the first cell to initialize the Azure ML workspace.

Initialize the workspace

```
# Config file already exist in compute instance
from azureml.core import Workspace

ws = Workspace.from_config()
print(ws.name, ws.resource_group, ws.location, ws.subscription_id, sep = '\n')
```
```
ADS_AMLworkspace
ADS_Book
westus2
```

Figure 5-4. *Azure ML workspace initialization*

If running on local, you would either need the config file (shown in Figure 5-1) or run the following code to pass the workspace information. The cell uses Python method os.getenv to read values from environment variables. If no environment variable exists, the parameters will be set to the specified default values.

If running on local, supply the below information from Azure ML workspace

```
import os

subscription_id = os.getenv("SUBSCRIPTION_ID", default="<my-subscription-id>")
resource_group = os.getenv("RESOURCE_GROUP", default="<my-resource-group>")
workspace_name = os.getenv("WORKSPACE_NAME", default="<my-workspace-name>")
workspace_region = os.getenv("WORKSPACE_REGION", default="eastus2")
```

Access your workspace

```
from azureml.core import Workspace

try:
    ws = Workspace(subscription_id = subscription_id, resource_group = resource_group,
                workspace_name = workspace_name)
    # write the details of the workspace to a configuration file to the notebook library
    ws.write_config()
    print("Workspace configuration succeeded. Skip the workspace creation steps below")
except:
    print("Workspace not accessible. Change your parameters or create a new workspace below")
```
```
Workspace configuration succeeded. Skip the workspace creation steps below
```

Figure 5-5. *Azure ML workspace access on local*

3.   Create an Experiment. The experiment will contain
your run records, experiment artifacts, and metrics
associated to the runs. Run the next cell and you
will see the output like the following with a link to
navigating to Azure ML Studio.

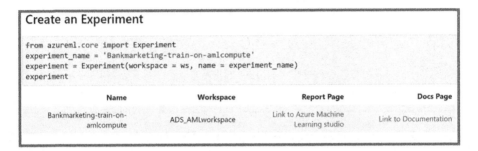

Figure 5-6. *Azure ML creating experiment*

Click the Report Page link to check the experiment
is created. Please note at this point you will see
no runs as we will define the run going forward
and submit it to the experiment. An experiment
can contain as many runs as user submits for the
purposes of experimenting, training, and testing the
models.

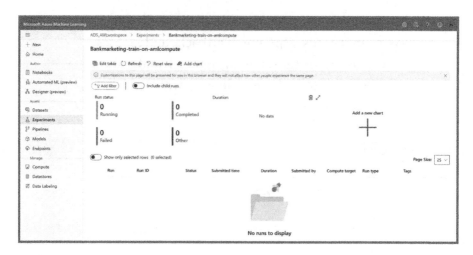

Figure 5-7. *Azure ML experiment on studio portal*

4. Next, we create Azure ML compute cluster for
    training. At the time of creation, the user needs to
    specify vm_size (family of VM nodes) and max_
    nodes to create a persistent compute resource. The
    compute autoscales down to zero node (default
    min_node= zero) when not in use, and max_node
    defines the number of nodes to autoscale up when
    running a job on cluster. Optionally, users can
    also specify vm_priority = 'lowpriority' to save the
    cost, but it's not recommended for training jobs on
    heavy data as these VMs do not have guaranteed
    availability and can be pre-empted while in use.
    Please run the next command to create compute
    cluster and wait for few minutes to be deployed.

Create Azure machine learning Compute clusters

```python
from azureml.core.compute import ComputeTarget, AmlCompute
from azureml.core.compute_target import ComputeTargetException

# Choose a name for your CPU cluster
cpu_cluster_name = "ninjacpucluster"

# Verify that cluster does not exist already
try:
    cpu_cluster = ComputeTarget(workspace=ws, name=cpu_cluster_name)
    print('Found existing cluster, use it.')
except ComputeTargetException:
    compute_config = AmlCompute.provisioning_configuration(vm_size='STANDARD_D2_V2',
                                                           max_nodes=4)
    cpu_cluster = ComputeTarget.create(ws, cpu_cluster_name, compute_config)

cpu_cluster.wait_for_completion(show_output=True)

Found existing cluster, use it.
Succeeded
AmlCompute wait for completion finished

Minimum number of nodes requested have been provisioned
```

Figure 5-8. *Azure ML compute clusters creation*

After the code finished running, you should be able to see the compute cluster created on the Azure ML Studio under Compute ➤ Compute clusters as well.

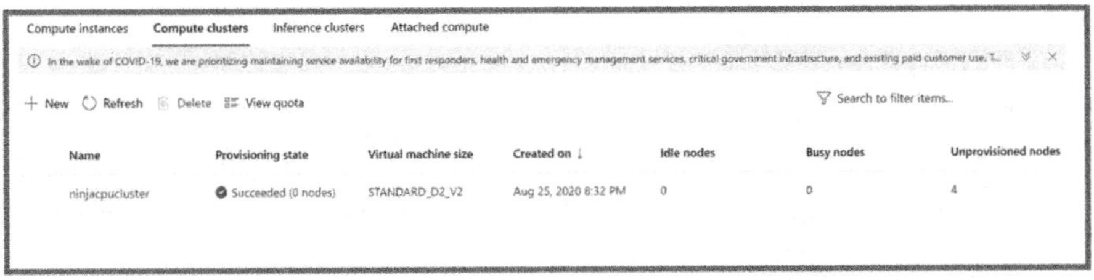

Name	Provisioning state	Virtual machine size	Created on ↓	Idle nodes	Busy nodes	Unprovisioned nodes
ninjacpucluster	✓ Succeeded (0 nodes)	STANDARD_D2_V2	Aug 25, 2020 8:32 PM	0	0	4

Figure 5-9. *Azure ML compute clusters on the portal*

5. Default/register new Datastores. Datastore is your
    data source, and dataset is your file/table/images
    in your data source. Azure ML has its storage
    account (created at the time of Azure ML workspace
    creation) as default datastore, but users can register
    preexisting data sources like Azure Blob Storage,
    Azure SQL DB, and so on as datastores as well.
    We will use default datastore in hands-on lab and
    upload bank marketing dataset to the datastore.
    Follow the next three cells to see all the registered
    datastores, default datastore, and create a new
    datastore.

Workspace Datastores ¶

```
datastores = ws.datastores
datastores

{'kaggledatabook': {
    "name": "kaggledatabook",
    "container_name": "opendata",
    "account_name": "kaggledatabook",
    "protocol": "https",
    "endpoint": "core.windows.net"
},
 'azureml_globaldatasets': {
    "name": "azureml_globaldatasets",
    "container_name": "globaldatasets",
    "account_name": "mmstoragewestus2",
    "protocol": "https",
    "endpoint": "core.windows.net"
},
 'opendata': {
    "name": "opendata",
    "container_name": "datasets",
    "account_name": "holstoragev2",
    "protocol": "https",
    "endpoint": "core.windows.net"
},
 'workspacefilestore': {
    "name": "workspacefilestore",
    "container_name": "azureml-filestore-6f61da3d-8d28-4c47-b40c-e2743511c301",
    "account_name": "adsamlworkspac8022875928",
    "protocol": "https",
    "endpoint": "core.windows.net"
},
```

Figure 5-10. *Azure ML workspace datastores*

Default datastore

```
datastore = ws.get_default_datastore()
datastore
```

```
{
  "name": "workspaceblobstore",
  "container_name": "azureml-blobstore-6f61da3d-8d28-4c47-b40c-e2743511c301",
  "account_name": "adsamlworkspac8022875928",
  "protocol": "https",
  "endpoint": "core.windows.net"
}
```

Figure 5-11. *Azure ML workspace default datastores*

Register a new datastore.

Register a new datastore

```
from azureml.core import Datastore
blob_datastore_name='kaggledatabook' # Name of the datastore to workspace
container_name=os.getenv("BLOB_CONTAINER", "opendata") # Name of Azure blob container
account_name=os.getenv("BLOB_ACCOUNTNAME", "kaggledatabook") # Storage account name
# Storage account access key
account_key=os.getenv("BLOB_ACCOUNT_KEY",
                      "QGmWeGNpXKFtmU7cnXW5Dg0LwX7L2SCbfjsZlBKKHHgsdhABgTfFo5Vh4ja3KTFdCfDrh7Q6n3SGpVlE4g/eXA==")

blob_datastore = Datastore.register_azure_blob_container(workspace=ws,
                                            datastore_name=blob_datastore_name,
                                            container_name=container_name,
                                            account_name=account_name,
                                            account_key=account_key)
blob_datastore
```

Figure 5-12. *Azure ML registration of new datastores*

6. Upload data to datastore to create a dataset or read existing data from datastore as a dataset. Dataset can be File or Tabular format; we will use Tabular Dataset as we are working with .csv. Run the next cells to upload data to Datastore and register the datasets in your workspace.

Upload data to datastore as dataset

```
blob_datastore.upload_files(files = ['./Bank.csv'], overwrite = True, show_progress = True)
```

```
Uploading an estimated of 1 files
Uploading ./Bank.csv
Uploaded ./Bank.csv, 1 files out of an estimated total of 1
Uploaded 1 files
$AZUREML_DATAREFERENCE_kaggledatabook
```

Read existing data from datastore as a dataset

```
from azureml.core.dataset import Dataset
bank_dataset = Dataset.Tabular.from_delimited_files(path=blob_datastore.path('Bank.csv'))
bank_dataset
```

```
{
  "source": [
    "('kaggledatabook', 'Bank.csv')"
  ],
  "definition": [
    "GetDatastoreFiles",
    "ParseDelimited",
    "DropColumns",
    "SetColumnTypes"
  ]
}
```

Figure 5-13. *Azure ML datasets*

Register the datasets in workspace to share with others and reuse in experiments

```
bank_ds = bank_dataset.register(workspace=ws,
                                name='bank_dataset',
                                description='Bank_Marketing_Kaggledata')
```

```
#Retrieve data from registered datasets
bank_ds = Dataset.get_by_name(ws, name='bank_dataset')
```

Figure 5-14. *Azure ML datasets*

Once you register, you should be able to see the dataset in Azure ML workspace portal as well like the following. Registered datasets keep track of data version and can be used in multiple experiments with code or designer by multiple users.

Figure 5-15. *Azure ML datasets studio view*

Now that we have done logistics setup, let's begin working on our specific use case in hand and build a machine learning model.

Note   For this hands-on lab, we will use Kaggle dataset as a source as mentioned earlier and predict if a client will subscribe to term deposit. The term deposit can be defined as a cash investment held at a financial institution at an agreed rate of interest over an agreed period of time. The dataset includes some features like age, job, marital status, education, default, housing, and so on which we will study and use in our experiment.

Training on remote cluster

To train the model on remote cluster, users need to submit the job to run as an experiment on a compute cluster. This process requires four components, and in the following, we will do hands-on building each of those components.

- Directory/folder

- Training script

- Estimator

- Model registration

1. **Create a Directory/folder.** A directory/folder is the key element of training as it contains all the necessary code, environment submitted from your development environment/local computer/ compute instance to the remote cluster, in our case Azure ML compute cluster. Run the next cell to create a folder.

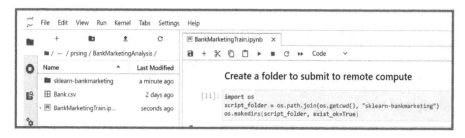

Figure 5-16. *Azure ML workspace script folder*

2. **Create a Training Script.** A training script contains all your code to train your model which gets submitted to Estimator class of experiment. This script should exist in the folder created in the last

step. For bank marketing campaign, we will train XgBoost machine learning model which is a very common machine learning classifier and will predict the results of campaigning. In training script

a. First, import all the necessary Python packages.

Create a Training Script

```
%%writefile $script_folder/train_bankmarketing.py

import os
import argparse
import pickle
import pandas as pd
from azureml.core import Dataset, Run
import numpy as np
from sklearn.metrics import accuracy_score #metrics
from sklearn.model_selection import train_test_split
from sklearn import model_selection
from sklearn.metrics import accuracy_score
from sklearn.preprocessing import LabelEncoder
from sklearn.ensemble import GradientBoostingClassifier

# sklearn.externals.joblib is removed in 0.23
from sklearn import __version__ as sklearnver
from packaging.version import Version
if Version(sklearnver) < Version("0.23.0"):
    from sklearn.externals import joblib
else:
    import joblib
```

Figure 5-17. Azure ML packages installation

b. Pass the parameters using "argparse" library to train
   the machine learning model like it's shown in the
   following. You can log parameters for each of your
   run to keep track of metrics and to reuse for future
   training of models. Here, we are logging parameters
   by using run.log() method.

```python
#Run object return current service context for logging metrics and uploading files
run = Run.get_context() |

def main():
    parser = argparse.ArgumentParser()
    parser.add_argument('--learning_rate', type=float, default=0.2,
                        help='learning_rate parameter to be used in the algorithm')
    parser.add_argument('--n_estimators', type=int, default=100,
                        help='n_estimators to be used in the algorithm')
    parser.add_argument('--max_depth', type=int, default=3,
                        help='max_depth parameter to be used in the algorithm')
    parser.add_argument('--min_samples_split', type=int, default=100,
                        help='min_samples_split to be used in the algorithm')
    parser.add_argument('--min_samples_leaf', type=int, default=100,
                        help='min_samples_leaf to be used in the algorithm')
    parser.add_argument('--subsample', type=float, default=3.0,
                        help='subsample parameter to be used in the algorithm')
    parser.add_argument('--random_state', type=float, default=0.7,
                        help='random_state to be used in the algorithm')
    parser.add_argument('--max_features', type=float, default=0.0,
                        help='max_features parameter to be used in the algorithm')


    args = parser.parse_args()
    run.log('learning_rate', np.float(args.learning_rate))
    run.log('n_estimators', np.int(args.n_estimators))
    run.log('max_depth', np.int(args.max_depth))
    run.log('min_samples_split', np.int(args.min_samples_split))
    run.log('min_samples_leaf', np.int(args.min_samples_leaf))
    run.log('subsample', np.float(args.subsample))
    run.log('random_state', np.int(args.random_state))
    run.log('max_features', np.int(args.max_features))
```

***Figure 5-18.** Experiment training script arguments*

c. After passing parameters, you retrieve the input data for your experiment. The training script reads an argument to find the directory that contains data. We will use input data using data folder parameters and pass it in the script. We can use Dataset object to mount or download the files referred by it. Usually mounting is faster than downloading as mounting loads files at the time of processing and exists as mount point, that is, a reference to the file system.

d. Next, users can combine Data Cleaning code and Model Training code, or they can create multiple experiments to keep track of these tasks individually. In this lab, we have combined both the tasks. Data Cleaning code includes changing the categorical values to numerical by using LabelEncoder or One Hot Encoding preprocessing SKlearn Python functions. Model Training code includes building the machine learning model, like for classification, we are using gradient boosting classifier. Other classifier/regressions methods can be used as well depending on the use case. The following is Data Cleaning code along with splitting it in train-test data.

```
# get input dataset by name
bank_dataset = run.input_datasets['bank_dataset']
data = bank_dataset.to_pandas_dataframe()


# Data Cleaning
cat_col = ['default', 'housing', 'loan', 'deposit', 'job',
           'marital', 'education', 'contact', 'month', 'poutcome']
for column in cat_col:
    label_encoder = LabelEncoder()
    label_encoder = label_encoder.fit(data[column])
    label_encoded_y = label_encoder.transform(data[column])
    data[column + '_cat'] = label_encoded_y
#     data[column + '_bool'] = data[column].eq('yes').mul(1)
data = data.drop(columns = cat_col)

#drop irrelevant columns
data = data.drop(columns = ['pdays'])
#impute incorrect values and drop original columns
def get_correct_values(row, column_name, threshold, df):
    ''' Returns mean value if value in column_name is above threshold'''
    if row[column_name] <= threshold:
        return row[column_name]
    else:
        mean = df[df[column_name] <= threshold][column_name].mean()
        return mean
data['campaign_cleaned'] = data.apply(lambda row: get_correct_values(row, 'campaign', 50, data),axis=1)
data['previous_cleaned'] = data.apply(lambda row: get_correct_values(row, 'previous', 50, data),axis=1)
data = data.drop(columns = ['campaign', 'previous'])
```

Figure 5-19. *Experiment training script for cleaning*

e. Lastly, we would put XGB Classifier code and fit our
   model on training data using the parameters passed.
   The training script includes the code to save the
   model in to directory named output folder in your
   run. All the content of this directory gets uploaded
   to the workspace automatically. We will retrieve
   our model from this directory in the next steps. The
   following is the code we will use to fit the model
   on bank marketing training data. Run the create
   training script cell to save the train_bankmarketing.
   py in script folder.

```
# Model Training
X = data.drop(columns = 'deposit_cat')
y = data[['deposit_cat']]

X_train, X_test, y_train, y_test = train_test_split(X, y, test_size = 0.15, seed = 300)
Params = {'learning_rate': np.float(args.learning_rate),
          'n_estimators': np.int(args.n_estimators),
          'max_depth': np.int(args.max_depth),
          'min_samples_split': np.int(args.min_samples_split),
          'min_samples_leaf': np.int(args.min_samples_leaf),
          'subsample': np.float(args.subsample),
          'random_state': np.int(args.random_state),
          'max_features': np.int(args.max_features)}

# GradientBoostingClassifier
clf = GradientBoostingClassifier(**Params)
clf.fit(X_train,y_train.squeeze().values)

#calculate and print scores for the model
y_train_preds = clf.predict(X_train)
y_test_preds = clf.predict(X_test)

model_file_name = 'joblibGB_bankmarketing.sav'
accuracy_score_train = accuracy_score(y_train, y_train_preds)
accuracy_score_test = accuracy_score(y_test, y_test_preds)
run.log('Gradient Boosting Accuracy Score for training', accuracy_score_train)
run.log('Graident Boosting Accuracy Score for testing', accuracy_score_test)

# Save the trained model
os.makedirs('outputs', exist_ok=True)
joblib.dump(value=clf, filename='outputs/' + model_file_name)

if __name__ == '__main__':
    main()
```

```
Overwriting /mnt/batch/tasks/shared/LS_root/mounts/clusters/adscompute/code/Users/prsing/BankMarketingAnalysi
s/sklearn-bankmarketing/train_bankmarketing.py
```

Figure 5-20. *Experiment training script for model building and logging arguments*

3. **Create an Estimator.** The estimator object is used to submit your run in the experiment. Azure ML includes pre-configured estimators for common machine learning frameworks like SKLearn, PyTorch, and generic estimators to be used for other frameworks. An estimator should include the following components to have successful run on remote compute:

   a. Name of estimator object, like est or estimator.

   b. Directory/folder that contains the code/scripts. All the content of this directory gets uploaded to the clusters for execution.

    c. Script parameters if any.

    d. The training script name, train_bankmarketing.py

    e. Input Dataset for training as_named_input, training script will use this reference for data.

    f. The compute target/remote compute. In our case, it's Azure ML compute cluster named "ninjacpucluster."

    g. Environment definition for the experiment.

Run the next cells to create a SKLearn estimator and submit the experiment. Users can add tags at this time to keep tag with their experiments for easy reference.

Create an Estimator

```
from azureml.train.sklearn import SKLearn
# from azureml.core import Dataset
script_params = {
    '--learning_rate': 0.01,
    '--n_estimators' : 600,
    '--max_depth': 9,
    '--min_samples_split': 1200,
    '--min_samples_leaf': 60,
    '--subsample': 0.85,
    '--random_state': 10,
    '--max_features': 7,
}

estimator = SKLearn(source_directory=script_folder,
            script_params=script_params,
            entry_script='train_bankmarketing.py',
            inputs=[bank_dataset.as_named_input('bank_dataset')],
            pip_packages=['azureml-dataset-runtime[fuse]', 'packaging', 'numpy==1.16.2'],
            compute_target=cpu_cluster_name)
```

```
run = experiment.submit(estimator)
run.tag("GB_BankMArketing_joblibsave")
```

```
from azureml.widgets import RunDetails

# monitor the run
RunDetails(run).show()
```

```
_UserRunWidget(widget_settings={'childWidgetDisplay': 'popup', 'send_telemetry': False, 'log_level': 'INFO',
…
```

Figure 5-21. *Azure ML experiment estimator*

Once we submit the experiment, we can use RunDetails to check the progress. We can also click the link to check the progress on Azure ML workspace portal.

Figure 5-22. *Azure ML experiment run details*

At this time, the following processes take place:

- The docker image is being created to develop Python environment specified in estimator. The first run takes longer than the subsequent runs as it's creating a docker image with the dependencies defined. Unless dependencies are changed, the subsequent runs use the same docker image. The image is uploaded to the workspace and can be seen in logs.

- Autoscaling happens if the remote cluster requires more nodes than available.

- Running the entry script on compute target and datastore/datasets mounting for input data.

- Preprocessing happens to copy the result of ./ output directory of the run from VM of the cluster to the run history in your workspace.

Once the run finishes, we will be able to retrieve metrics logged in our experiment. This creates a testing environment for users to experiment/ develop a good model and keep track of experiments. Once a satisfactory performance is achieved, users can go ahead and register the model. Use the following command to retrieve parameters, model performance, and so on.

```
run.get_metrics()

{'learning_rate': 0.01,
 'n_estimators': 600,
 'max_depth': 9,
 'min_samples_split': 1200,
 'min_samples_leaf': 60,
 'subsample': 0.85,
 'random_state': 10,
 'max_features': 7,
 'Gradient Boosting Accuracy Score for training': 0.8597027511331296,
 'Graident Boosting Accuracy Score for testing': 0.84}

print(run.get_file_names())

['azureml-logs/55_azureml-execution-tvmps_73e594ac5d530258c5ff9c0d0bc24f2333effc4a52fb720e28fccae062be894a_d.
txt', 'azureml-logs/65_job_prep-tvmps_73e594ac5d530258c5ff9c0d0bc24f2333effc4a52fb720e28fccae062be894a_d.tx
t', 'azureml-logs/70_driver_log.txt', 'azureml-logs/75_job_post-tvmps_73e594ac5d530258c5ff9c0d0bc24f2333effc4
a52fb720e28fccae062be894a_d.txt', 'azureml-logs/process_info.json', 'azureml-logs/process_status.json', 'log
s/azureml/108_azureml.log', 'logs/azureml/dataprep/backgroundProcess.log', 'logs/azureml/dataprep/backgroundP
rocess_Telemetry.log', 'logs/azureml/dataprep/engine_spans_l_bede9d3b-6b69-4ea2-a160-48356d1d9559.jsonl', 'lo
gs/azureml/dataprep/python_span_l_bede9d3b-6b69-4ea2-a160-48356d1d9559.jsonl', 'logs/azureml/job_prep_azurem
l.log', 'logs/azureml/job_release_azureml.log', 'outputs/joblibGB_bankmarketing.sav']
```

Figure 5-23. *Azure ML experiment metrics*

4. **Register the model.** This is the last step in Model Training life cycle. After running the experiment step, our model.pkl will exist in the run records of experiments in workspace. The model registry contains your trained models and is accessible to other users in workspace. Once the model is registered with version number, later it can be used to query, examine, deploy, and for MLOps purposes (refer to Chapter8). Run the next cell to register the model.

Register the moodel

```
# register model
model = run.register_model(model_name='Gradientboosting_bankmarketing',
                           model_path='outputs/Gradientboosting_bankmarketing.pkl')
print(model.name, model.id, model.version, sep='\t')
```

```
Gradientboosting_bankmarketing  Gradientboosting_bankmarketing:1        1
```

Figure 5-24. *Azure ML model registration*

Note   The model can come from Azure ML or from somewhere else. While registering the model, the path of either a cloud location or local directory is provided. The path is used to locate the model files to upload as a registration process.

After running the preceding cell, we will be able to see our registered model on the Azure ML workspace like the following.

Figure 5-25. *Azure ML model on studio portal*

Deploying your model as web service

Deploying your model as a web service simply means creating a docker image that captures machine learning model, scoring logic, and its authentication parameters. We will now go ahead and deploy our model on Azure container instance (ACI). Container instance runs docker containers on-demand in a managed, serverless Azure environment. It's an easy solution to test the deployment performance, scoring workflow, and debug issues. Once the deploy model workflow is built, we would deploy the model to Azure Kubernetes Service for more scalable production environment. Refer to Chapter 4 to understand the suitable service for deployments.

Deploying the model to Azure container instance (ACI), Azure Kubernetes Service (AKS), or in general compute targets requires three basic components:

- **Scoring script** to understand the model workflow and run the model to return the prediction

- **Configuration file** to define the environment/software dependencies needed for deployment

- **Deployment configuration** to define characteristics of compute target to host the model and scoring script

For the purposes of this lab, we will first deploy on Azure container instance, do some testing, and later will deploy on Azure Kubernetes Service (AKS). So, let's go ahead and create a scoring script for our bank marketing model.

1. **Create Scoring Script.** This script is specific to your model and should incorporate data format/ schema expected by the model. The script will receive the data submitted to the web service, pass it to the registered model, and return the response/ predictions. Scoring Script requires two functions:

a. Init(): This function is called when the service is initialized and loads your model in a global object.

b. Run(rawdata): This function is called when the new data is submitted and uses the model loaded in init() function to make the predictions.

Run the next cell to create the scoring script for our use case.

Create Scoring Script

```
%%writefile score.py
import json
import numpy as np
import os
import pickle
from sklearn.externals import joblib
from sklearn import __version__ as sklearnver
from packaging.version import Version
if Version(sklearnver) < Version("0.23.0"):
    from sklearn.externals import joblib
else:
    import joblib
from azureml.core.model import Model

def init():
    global model
    # AZUREML_MODEL_DIR is an environment variable created during deployment.
    # It is the path to the model folder (./azureml-models/$MODEL_NAME/$VERSION)
    # For multiple models, it points to the folder containing all deployed models (./azureml-models)
    model_filename = 'joblibGB_bankmarketing.sav'
    model_path = os.path.join(os.environ['AZUREML_MODEL_DIR'], model_filename)
    model = joblib.load(model_path)

def run(raw_data):
    data = np.array(json.loads(raw_data)['data'])
    # make prediction
    y_hat = model.predict(data)
    # you can return any data type as long as it is JSON-serializable
    return y_hat.tolist()
```
Overwriting score.py

Figure 5-26. *Azure ML scoring script*

2. **Configuration File.** This file includes model's
   runtime environment in Environment object and
   CondaDependencies needed by your model. Make
   sure to pass specific versions of Python libraries
   used while training the model. Run the next cell to
   create configuration file.

```python
from azureml.core import Environment
from azureml.core.conda_dependencies import CondaDependencies
import sklearn

environment = Environment('my-sklearn-environment')
environment.python.conda_dependencies = CondaDependencies.create(pip_packages=[
    'azureml-defaults',
    'inference-schema[numpy-support]',
    'joblib',
    'numpy==1.16.2',
    'packaging',
    'scikit-learn=={}'.format(sklearn.__version__)
])
```

Figure 5-27. *Azure ML environment configuration file*

3. **Deployment Configuration.** This configuration is
   required to create the docker image specific to the
   compute target. We will be deploying our model
   to Azure container instance (ACI) first for testing
   purposes. Run the following code to deploy your
   model to ACI. This process will take 5–10 minutes
   or longer depending on model trained and software
   dependencies.

```
from azureml.core.model import InferenceConfig
from azureml.core.webservice import AciWebservice


service_name = 'joblibgb-bankmarketing'

inference_config = InferenceConfig(entry_script='score.py', environment=environment)
aci_config = AciWebservice.deploy_configuration(cpu_cores=1, memory_gb=1)

service = Model.deploy(workspace=ws,
                       name=service_name,
                       models=[model],
                       inference_config=inference_config,
                       deployment_config=aci_config,
                       overwrite=True)
service.wait_for_deployment(show_output=True)
Running.........................
Succeeded
ACI service creation operation finished, operation "Succeeded"
```

Figure 5-28. *Azure ML deployment configuration on Azure container instance*

```
service.get_logs()

'2020-08-29T15:41:54,583695133+00:00 - iot-server/run \n2020-08-29T15:41:54,586339411+00:00 - nginx/run \n2
020-08-29T15:41:54,587586701+00:00 - rsyslog/run \n/usr/sbin/nginx: /azureml-envs/azureml_032341806dd16cc7d
4cebbeb5ef1817c/lib/libcrypto.so.1.0.0: no version information available (required by /usr/sbin/nginx)\n/us
r/sbin/nginx: /azureml-envs/azureml_032341806dd16cc7d4cebbeb5ef1817c/lib/libcrypto.so.1.0.0: no version inf
ormation available (required by /usr/sbin/nginx)\n/usr/sbin/nginx: /azureml-envs/azureml_032341806dd16cc7d4
cebbeb5ef1817c/lib/libssl.so.1.0.0: no version information available (required by /usr/sbin/nginx)\n/usr/sb
in/nginx: /azureml-envs/azureml_032341806dd16cc7d4cebbeb5ef1817c/lib/libssl.so.1.0.0: no version informatio
n available (required by /usr/sbin/nginx)\n/usr/sbin/nginx: /azureml-envs/azureml_032341806dd16cc7d4cebbeb5
ef1817c/lib/libssl.so.1.0.0: no version information available (required by /usr/sbin/nginx)\n2020-08-29T15:
41:54,583315136+00:00 - gunicorn/run \nEdgeHubConnectionString and IOTEDGE_IOTHUBHOSTNAME are not set. Exit
ing...\n2020-08-29T15:41:54,782075687+00:00 - iot-server/finish 1 0\n2020-08-29T15:41:54,783433576+00:00 -
Exit code 1 is normal. Not restarting iot-server.\nStarting gunicorn 19.9.0\nListening at: http://127.0.0.
1:31311 (14)\nUsing worker: sync\nworker timeout is set to 300\nBooting worker with pid: 42\nInitialized Py
Spark session.\nInitializing logger\nStarting up app insights client\nStarting up request id generator\nSta
rting up app insight hooks\nInvoking user\'s init function\nUsers\'s init has completed successfully\nSkipp
ing middleware: dbg_model_info as it\'s not enabled.\nScoring timeout is found from os.environ: 60000 ms\nS
wagger file not present\n404\n127.0.0.1 - - [29/Aug/2020:15:42:05 +0000] "GET /swagger.json HTTP/1.0" 404 1
9 "-" "Go-http-client/1.1"\nSwagger file not present\n404\n127.0.0.1 - - [29/Aug/2020:15:42:07 +0000] "GET
/swagger.json HTTP/1.0" 404 19 "-" "Go-http-client/1.1"\nSwagger file not present\n404\n127.0.0.1 - - [29/A
ug/2020:15:42:23 +0000] "GET /swagger.json HTTP/1.0" 404 19 "-" "Go-http-client/1.1"\n'

print(service.scoring_uri)

http://764223ca-901a-4b72-be70-7ec48213d18f.westus2.azurecontainer.io/score
```

Figure 5-29. *Azure ML deploy logs*

If deployment fails for multiple reasons, use commands shown in Figure 5-29 to get the logs for troubleshooting purposes. Once the service deployment is succeeded, we will be able to retrieve our scoring URL using the service.scoring_uri shown in Figure 5-29.

Now, we will perform a quick testing to see if we can score using our test data. Run the next cell to see the prediction for term deposit retrieved from web service.

```python
import pandas as pd
import requests
import json

df_list = X_test.values.tolist()
data = {}
data['data'] = df_list
input_data = json.dumps(data)

# Set the content type
# # If authentication is enabled, set the authorization header
# headers['Authorization'] = f'Bearer {key}'
headers = {'Content-Type': 'application/json'}

# Make the request and display the response
resp = requests.post(scoring_uri, input_data, headers=headers)
# resp_json = resp.text
X_test['pred_termdeposit'] = resp.json()
# retrieve first 10 predictions from the response
resp.json()[:10]
```
```
[1, 1, 0, 0, 1, 0, 1, 1, 1, 0]
```

Figure 5-30. *Azure ML deployed model web service test*

Now that we have tested the model deployed as web service on ACI, we would go ahead and deploy on Azure Kubernetes Service (AKS). First, let's create an AKS cluster, run the following code to create the AKS cluster: it will take a few minutes to create the cluster.

```
Deploy on Azure Kubernetes Service

Create AKS Cluster

from azureml.core.compute import AksCompute, ComputeTarget

prov_config = AksCompute.provisioning_configuration(vm_size = "STANDARD_DS3_V2",
                                                     agent_count = 1,
                                                     location = "westus2",
                                                     cluster_purpose = AksCompute.ClusterPurpose.DEV_TEST)

aks_name = 'myaks'
# Creates the cluster
aks_target = ComputeTarget.create(workspace = ws,
                                  name = aks_name,
                                  provisioning_configuration = prov_config)

# Waits for the create process to complete
aks_target.wait_for_completion(show_output = True)

Creating......................................................
SucceededProvisioning operation finished, operation "Succeeded"
```

Figure 5-31. *Azure Kubernetes cluster creation*

Note   Users can attach the existing AKS cluster as well. While creating or attaching, `cluster_purpose` defines the minimum virtual CPUs/GPUs required. For cluster_purpose = Dev_Test, at least 2 virtual CPUs are recommended; for cluster_purpose = Fast_PROD, at least 12 virtual CPUs are recommended.

We will use the same environment/configuration file as we used for ACI and deploy the model using AKS deploy configuration. Run the next cell to deploy the model on AKS.

```
Deploy

from azureml.core.webservice import AksWebservice, Webservice
from azureml.core.model import Model
from azureml.core.compute import AksCompute

aks_target = AksCompute(ws,cluster_name)
aks_target

AksCompute(workspace=Workspace.create(name='ADS_AMLworkspace', subscription_id='ab8f5415-63b3-4fd4-8a8a-92
13316abb6e', resource_group='ADS_Book'), name=myaks, id=/subscriptions/ab8f5415-63b3-4fd4-8a8a-9213316abb6
e/resourceGroups/ADS_Book/providers/Microsoft.MachineLearningServices/workspaces/ADS_AMLworkspace/compute
s/myaks, type=AKS, provisioning_state=Succeeded, location=westus2, tags=None)

deployment_config = AksWebservice.deploy_configuration(cpu_cores = 1, memory_gb = 1)
model = Model(ws, name='Gradientboosting_bankmarketing', version= 5)
service = Model.deploy(ws, "gb-bankmarketing", [model], inference_config, deployment_config, aks_target)
service.wait_for_deployment(show_output = True)
|

Running........
Succeeded
AKS service creation operation finished, operation "Succeeded"
```

Figure 5-32. *Azure ML deployment configuration on Azure Kubernetes Service*

Wait for a few minutes while deployment is in process; meanwhile, grab another coffee for the next tutorial on Automated Machine Learning (AutoML), a faster and easier way of building machine learning models. Once the code succeeds, we will be able to see our web service endpoints on Azure ML workspace portal like the following.

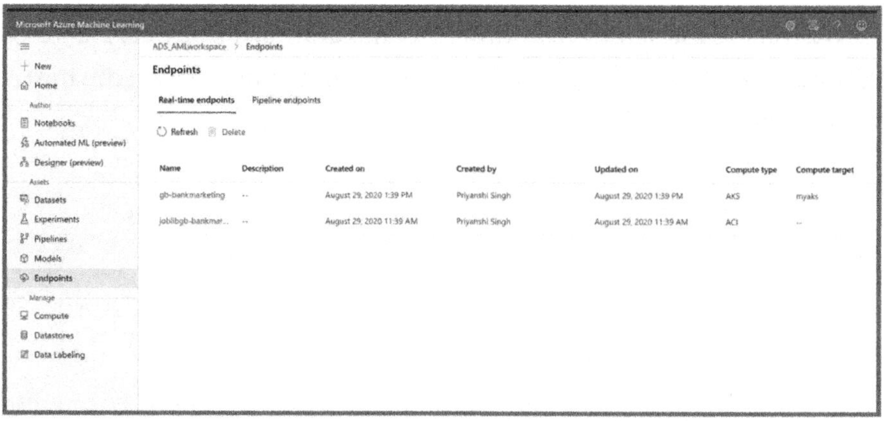

Figure 5-33. *Azure ML deployed models as web services*

Automated Machine Learning (AutoML)

Automated Machine Learning is a technique to design probabilistic machine learning models to automate experimental decisions while building models and optimizing performance. It allows users to try multiple algorithms, their hyperparameters tuning, and preprocessing transformations on your data combined with scalable cloud-based compute offerings. The automated process of finding the best performing model based on primary metric saves huge amount of time spent in manual trial and error processes. The goal of introducing AutoML is to accelerate and simplify artificial intelligence processes for a wider audience including data scientists, data engineers, business users, and developers. With AutoML, data scientists can automate part of their workflow and focus on other more important aspects of business objectives, while business users who don't have advanced data science and machine learning/coding expertise can benefit from AutoML user interface and build out models in minutes.

Users can begin with Automated Machine Learning by evaluating the following questions:

1. Identify ML problem:

   a. Classification

   b. Regression

   c. Forecasting

2. Python Azure ML SDK or Azure ML Studio: AutoML studio is available only in enterprise edition. The following is a comparison of features supported in both.

Model settings

These settings can be applied to the best model as a result of your automated ML experiment.

	The Python SDK	The studio web experience
Best model registration, deployment, explainability	✓	✓
Enable voting ensemble & stack ensemble models	✓	✓
Show best model based on non-primary metric	✓	
Enable/disable ONNX model compatibility	✓	
Test the model	✓	

Run control settings

These settings allow you to review and control your experiment runs and its child runs.

	The Python SDK	The studio web experience
Run summary table	✓	✓
Cancel runs & child runs	✓	✓
Get guardrails	✓	✓
Pause & resume runs	✓	

Experiment settings

The following settings allow you to configure your automated ML experiment.

	The Python SDK	The studio web experience
Split data into train/validation sets	✓	✓
Supports ML tasks: classification, regression, and forecasting	✓	✓
Optimizes based on primary metric	✓	✓
Supports AML compute as compute target	✓	✓
Configure forecast horizon, target lags & rolling window	✓	✓
Set exit criteria	✓	✓
Set concurrent iterations	✓	✓
Drop columns	✓	✓
Block algorithms	✓	✓
Cross validation	✓	✓
Supports training on Azure Databricks clusters	✓	
View engineered feature names	✓	
Featurization summary	✓	
Featurization for holidays	✓	
Log file verbosity levels	✓	

Figure 5-34. *Azure ML Studio vs. Azure ML SDK features. Source:*
`https://docs.microsoft.com/en-us/azure/machine-learning/`
`concept-automated-ml#parity`

For purposes of hands-on lab on AutoML, we will use the same bank marketing dataset and develop a classification model to predict the term deposit using both web and Python SDK. So let's go ahead and build our experiment using AutoML studio web experience and Python SDK.

AutoML studio web

We will use the Datastore and Dataset created earlier in this chapter and configure the experiment on the portal. AutoML supports automatic featurization to do standard preprocessing for the underlying model. Featurization steps like handling missing data, normalizing features, converting categorical values to numeric values, and so on are handled using various standard algorithms. These featurization steps are applied automatically to your data while making predictions as well as training process to keep the featurization consistent. Users are also allowed to do customized featurization by turning featurization "off" both on UI and in code. So let's go ahead and perform the following steps to train our model using AutoML UI:

1. Click the new Automated ML run as shown in Figure 5-35.

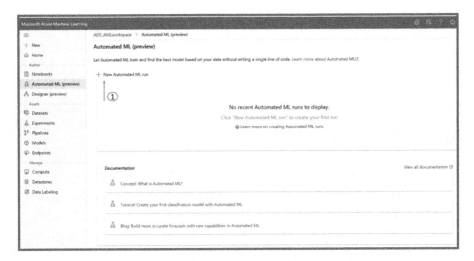

Figure 5-35. *AutoML on Azure ML Studio*

2. Next, we will use the Dataset created earlier. Users can also create a new dataset at this point from the following available options.

Figure 5-36. *AutoML experiment*

A good use case will be to include open dataset like
weather or census. Azure ML offers a variety of open
datasets.

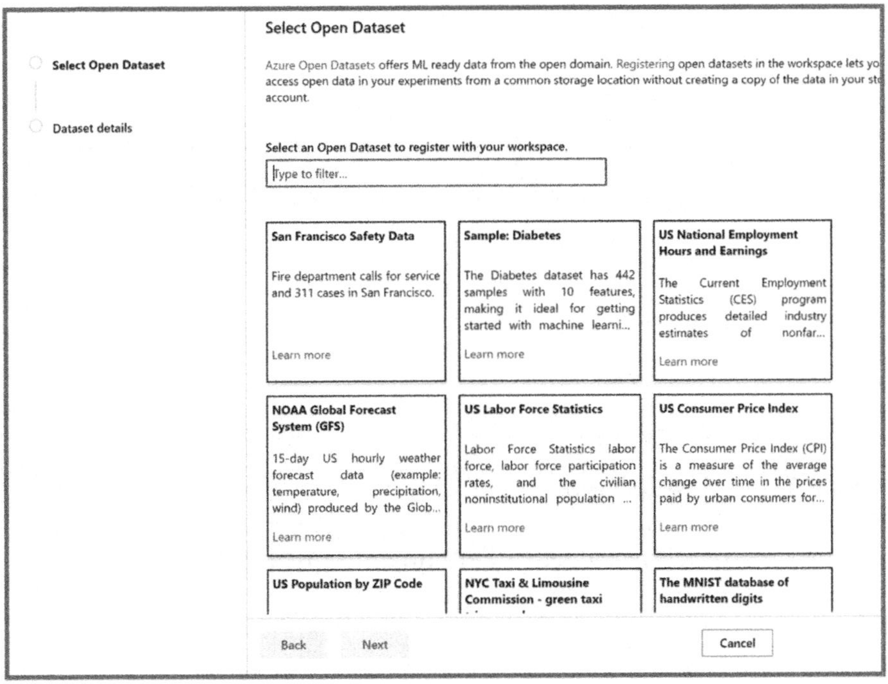

Figure 5-37. *Azure open datasets*

We will use bank dataset created previously (in this chapter) and will do a quick preview by clicking preview tab. Click Next after done previewing to continue with AutoML experiment.

age	job	marital	education	default	balance	housing	loan	contact	day	mo...	duration	campaign	pdays
59	ad...	married	secondary	no	2343	yes	no	unknown	5	may	1042	1	-1
56	ad...	married	secondary	no	45	no	no	unknown	5	may	1467	1	-1
41	te...	married	secondary	no	1270	yes	no	unknown	5	may	1389	1	-1
55	se...	married	secondary	no	2476	yes	no	unknown	5	may	579	1	-1
54	ad...	married	tertiary	no	184	no	no	unknown	5	may	673	2	-1
42	m...	single	tertiary	no	0	yes	yes	unknown	5	may	562	2	-1
56	m...	married	tertiary	no	830	yes	yes	unknown	6	may	1201	1	-1

bank_dataset — Data preview, Data statistics

Figure 5-38. *AutoML data preview*

3. Next, we will configure Experiment settings. Click Next.

Figure 5-39. *AutoML experiment configure*

4. At this step, we will pick classification for our use
    case. Users can enable deep learning option as well
    to incorporate deep learning models in machine
    learning algorithms, but it will take more time to
    finish the experiment.

Figure 5-40. *AutoML task identification*

We can also configure additional settings to change the default primary
metric, block any particular algorithms not to be used in experimentation,
and pick cross-validation like K-fold or Monte Carlo. For this hands-on lab,
we will leave everything to default.

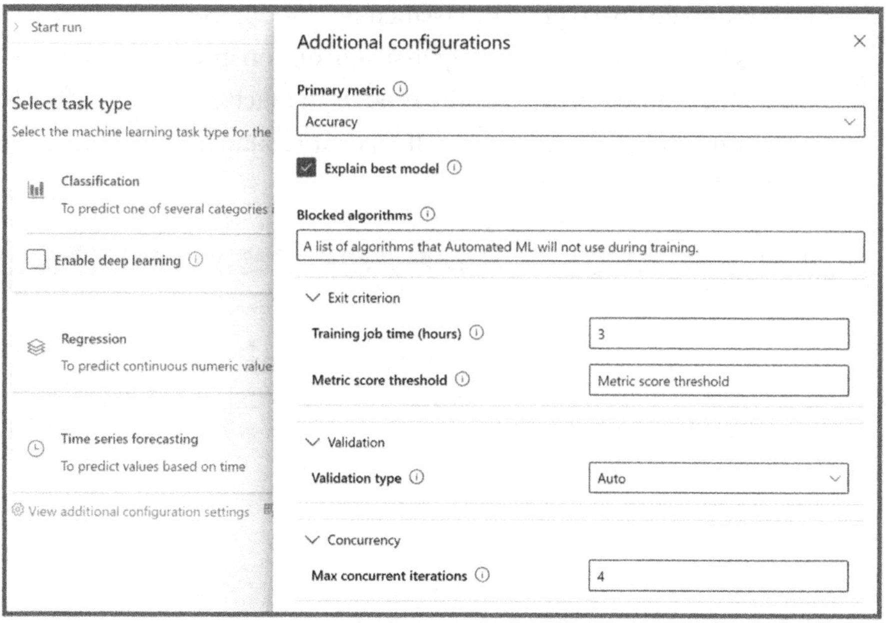

Figure 5-41. *AutoML additional configuration settings*

Users can also control additional features here. We will check off pdays at this point (shown in Figure 5-42) and click Save.

We will be returned to the previous screen (shown in Figure 5-40), and we will click Finish. Wait for experiment to run and finish; it will take 15 minutes or so depending on experiment configuration. Once the run is finished, we should be able to see our run details in experiment like the following

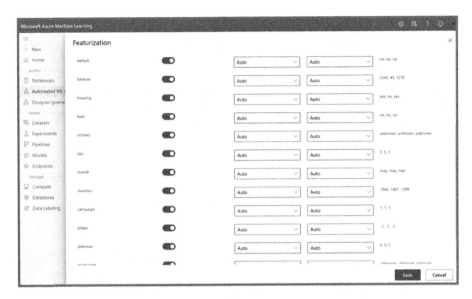

Figure 5-42. *AutoML additional featurization settings*

Figure 5-43. *AutoML experiment run details*

Note the resulting accuracy, the time it took to run the whole experiment, task, and other artifacts. Next, we will check what is the best-fitted model. Click Models, and we should be able to see our models.

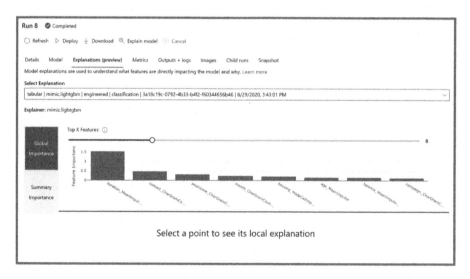

Figure 5-44. *AutoML models*

By clicking the Model-view explanation, we can view the feature importance as well.

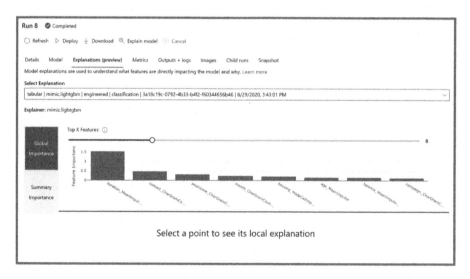

Figure 5-45. *AutoML feature explanations*

Users can explore other model metrics as well by clicking Metrics section.

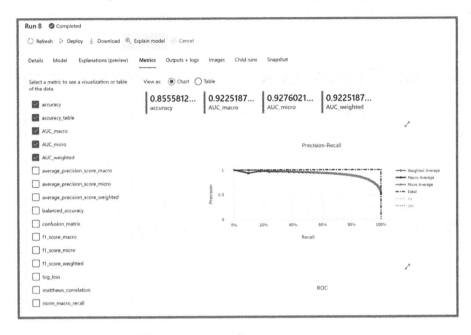

Figure 5-46. *AutoML metrics results*

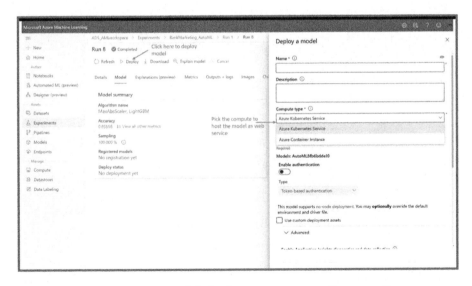

Figure 5-47. *AutoML model deployment on studio portal*

Next, we will deploy the model. Users can deploy the model on either ACI or AKS from the portal itself by first selecting the model and clicking Deploy (shown in Figure 5-47).

AutoML Python SDK

From all the previous datastore/dataset setup, we will go ahead and start writing code in JupyterLab to create an AutoML experiment in Python SDK.

Note   This hands-on lab will use previous prerequisite setup. If you've not run Azure ML SDK lab and doing AutoML lab, please run through the prerequisite setup section before starting this lab.

```
SetUp

import logging

from matplotlib import pyplot as plt
import pandas as pd
import os

import azureml.core
from azureml.core.experiment import Experiment
from azureml.core.workspace import Workspace
from azureml.core.automl.core.featurization import FeaturizationConfig
from azureml.core.dataset import Dataset
from azureml.train.automl import AutoMLConfig
from azureml.interpret._internal.explanation_client import ExplanationClient


Connect to AML workspace and create an experiment

ws = Workspace.from_config()

# choose a name for experiment
experiment_name = 'automlbankmarketing'

experiment=Experiment(ws, experiment_name)

output = {}
output['Subscription ID'] = ws.subscription_id
output['Workspace'] = ws.name
output['Resource Group'] = ws.resource_group
output['Location'] = ws.location
output['Experiment Name'] = experiment.name
pd.set_option('display.max_colwidth', -1)
outputDf = pd.DataFrame(data = output, index = [''])
outputDf.T
```

Subscription ID	ab8f5415-63b3-4fd4-8a8a-9213316abb6e
Workspace	ADS_AMLworkspace

Figure 5-48. *AutoML Python SDK setup*

1. Create a Jupyter notebook and put the code shown in Figure 5-48. To follow along with the code, users can also Git clone the repository from GitHub. To do that, refer to the following location. We will be using Automl_bankmarketing.ipynb notebook for the code.

   ```
   https://github.com/singh-soh/
   AzureDataScience/tree/master/Chapter05_
   AzureML_Part2
   ```

2. Run the cells to set up with libraries and connect to Azure ML workspace and instantiate an experiment.

3. Run the next cell to create a new/or use a previously created compute target. We will use previously created "ninjacpucluster" to create AutoML experiment (shown in Figure 5-49).

Create Azure machine learning Compute clusters

```python
from azureml.core.compute import ComputeTarget, AmlCompute
from azureml.core.compute_target import ComputeTargetException

# Choose a name for your CPU cluster
cpu_cluster_name = "ninjacpucluster"

# Verify that cluster does not exist already
try:
    cpu_cluster = ComputeTarget(workspace=ws, name=cpu_cluster_name)
    print('Found existing cluster, use it.')
except ComputeTargetException:
    compute_config = AmlCompute.provisioning_configuration(vm_size='STANDARD_D2_V2',
                                                           max_nodes=4)
    cpu_cluster = ComputeTarget.create(ws, cpu_cluster_name, compute_config)

cpu_cluster.wait_for_completion(show_output=True)
```
```
Found existing cluster, use it.
Succeeded
AmlCompute wait for completion finished

Minimum number of nodes requested have been provisioned
```

Figure 5-49. *AutoML Python SDK compute cluster*

4. Next, let's load the data from previously created 'bank_Dataset'. We will also split data into training and testing at this point.

Load data from bank_Dataset

```
bankdata = Dataset.get_by_name(ws, name='bank_dataset')
# bandata = dataset.to_pandas_dataframe()  # convert to dataframe
```

Split data into Training and Testing

```
training_data, validation_data = bankdata.random_split(percentage=0.8, seed=223)
label_column_name = 'deposit'
```

Figure 5-50. *AutoML Python SDK dataset and train/test split*

5. Next, we will configure AutoML settings. These settings define how your AutoML experiment will be run on what compute. Run the next cell to configure these settings.

Configure AutoML settings

```
automl_settings = {
    "experiment_timeout_hours" : 3,
    "enable_early_stopping" : True,
    "iteration_timeout_minutes": 5,
    "max_concurrent_iterations": 4,
    "max_cores_per_iteration": -1,
    #"n_cross_validations": 2,|
    "primary_metric": 'AUC_weighted',
    "featurization": 'auto',
    "verbosity": logging.INFO,
}

automl_config = AutoMLConfig(task = 'classification',
                             debug_log = 'automl_errors.log',
                             compute_target=compute_target,
                             experiment_exit_score = 0.9984,
                             blocked_models = ['KNN','LinearSVM'],
#                              enable_onnx_compatible_models=True,
                             training_data = training_data,
                             label_column_name = label_column_name,
                             **automl_settings
                            )
```

Figure 5-51. *AutoML Python SDK configuration settings*

The following is a short list of settings users can configure while running the experiment in Python SDK. For complete list, refer to detailed explanation here: https://docs.microsoft. com/en-us/python/api/azureml-train-automl-client/azureml.train.automl.automlconfig. automlconfig?view=azure-ml-py

a. task: Regression or classification or forecasting.

b. compute_target: Remote cluster/machine this experiment will use to create the run.

c. Primary_metric: Models are optimized based on this metric.

d. Experiment_exit_score: Value indicating the target of primary metric.

e. Blocked_models: User-specified models that will be ignored in training.

f. Training_data: Input dataset including features and label column.

g. Label_column_name: Target variable that needs to be predicted.

h. Experiment_timeout_hours: Maximum amount of time an experiment can take to terminate all the iterations.

i. Enable_early_stopping: Flag to enable early termination if the score is not improving in the iterations short term.

j. Iteration_timeout_minutes: Maximum time in minutes that each iteration can run before it terminates. Here, an iteration is total number of different algorithms and parameter combinations to test for AutoML experiment.

k. Max_concurrent_iterations: Maximum iterations executed in parallel.

l. Max_cores_per_iteration: Maximum number of threads to use for an iteration.

m. Featurization: Auto or off to determine if featurization should be done automatically or not or if customized featurization will be used.

6. After AutoI config settings, we would go ahead and submit the experiment to find the best-fitted model for our bank marketing prediction. You can track this experiment by following the link to Azure ML portal workspace; it will take 15–20 minutes to finish running. Run the next cell to submit the experiment.

Submit the experiment

```
remote_run = experiment.submit(automl_config, show_output = False)
Running on remote or ADB.

remote_run
```

Experiment	Id	Type	Status	Details Page	Docs Page
automlbankmarketing	AutoML_e56af6f2-48e3-4a15-8840-4bf893d21774	automl	NotStarted	Link to Azure Machine Learning studio	Link to Documentation

Figure 5-52. *AutoML Python SDK experiment*

7. Once it's completed, we will be able to retrieve the best-fitted model by following this command.

Get the best fitted model

```
best_run, fitted_model = remote_run.get_output()
fitted_model

PipelineWithYTransformations(Pipeline={'memory': None, 'steps': [('datatransformer', DataTransformer(enable_dnn=None, enable_feat
ure_sweeping=None,
        feature_sweeping_config=None, feature_sweeping_timeout=None,
        featurization_config=None, force_text_dnn=None,
        is_cross_validation=None, is_onnx_compatible=Non...66666666667, 0.06666666666666667, 0.06666666666666667, 0.0666666666666
6667, 0.06666666666666667]))],
        y_transformer={}, y_transformer_name='LabelEncoder')
```

Figure 5-53. *AutoML Python SDK best-fitted model retrieved*

8. We will be able to see the finished run on the portal as well along with best model trained considering the primary metric defined.

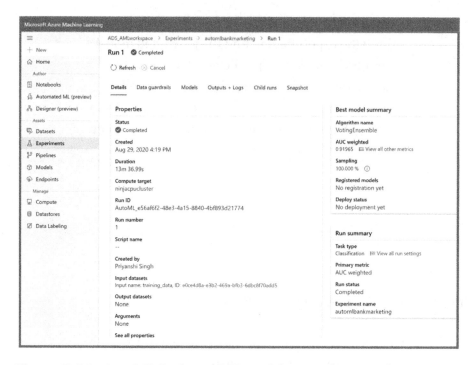

Figure 5-54. *AutoML Python SDK model on studio portal*

Note   The resulting model is different in both the methods –
AutoML on portal and AutoML on Python SDK. This is primarily due to
the different primary metric used along with different configurations.
However, users can always look into the metrics score by clicking
"View all other metrics."

9. Next step will be to register the best-fitted model
    and deploy it. These steps are the same as Azure
    ML Python SDK experiment done before; refer to
    the same code to deploy this model. To register the
    model, run the next command.

```
Register the best fitted model

model_name = best_run.properties['model_name']
description = 'AutoML Model trained on bank marketing data to predict if a client will subscribe to a term deposit'
tags = None
model = remote_run.register_model(model_name = model_name, description = description, tags = tags)
```

Figure 5-55. *AutoML Python SDK model registration*

Summary

In this chapter, we were able to do hands-on using Azure ML Python SDK with bank marketing dataset, logging metrics, model versions, and how to deploy the model to Azure container instance (ACI) and Azure Kubernetes Service (AKS). We also learned Automated Machine Learning (AutoML) using portal as well as Python SDK. There are several use cases for which Azure Machine Learning can be used. This chapter gives users a good understanding and hands-on experience to Azure ML, and users are encouraged to keep learning and explore ways to leverage ML on Azure whether on local computer or Azure Databricks workspace or Azure ML compute instance or a data science virtual machine. Please refer to this repo for plenty of resources and material to keep learning: `https:// github.com/singh-soh/AzureDataScience/tree/master/Chapter05_ AzureML_Part2`. To manage ML production life cycle, we will learn about Azure ML pipelines and ML operations in Chapter 8 and understand how to automate the workflows and follow Continuous Integration/Continuous Delivery (CI/CD) principles.

CHAPTER 6

Apache Spark, Big Data, and Azure Databricks

The exponential pace of innovation in artificial intelligence in recent years can be attributed to advancements in machine learning. In turn, the advancements in machine learning are based on two core developments – availability of data and ubiquitous access to unparalleled compute capabilities.

In Chapter 2 and elsewhere in this book, you have seen the recurring theme that the more data that is available to train models, the better the models are at predicting outcomes and help us make better decisions. The term "human parity" has been used as a benchmark to compare specific AI capabilities to those of a human being. We are at the point now where core capabilities like language translation, vision, and speech have surpassed human parity.

Big Data

Big Data is the term used to describe the phenomenon of data explosion. Data explosion can be attributed to multiple characteristics – the frequency (speed), volume, variety, and size. In recent years, these data characteristics have grown significantly and are expected to continue doing so.

The reason for this phenomenon is not only because of technological improvements but also the evolving and changing relationship of society with technology.

So how much data is this Big Data phenomenon? It is represented in terms of zettabytes (ZB), which is 1 billion terabytes. The forecast is 175ZB by the year 2025. Figure 6-1 is the chart presented by International Data Corporation (IDC),[1] who specialize in the analysis of global trends in technology.

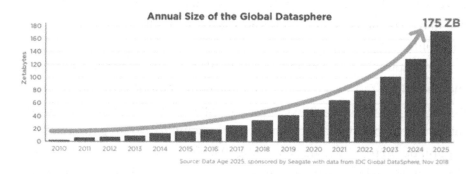

Figure 6-1. *IDC's forecast of global data growth through 2025*

---

[1]www.idc.com/about

Still unable to visualize the magnitude of 175ZB? Not to worry, so are we. As such, consider the following quote from IDC's Senior VP, David Reinsel:

> *If one were able to store 175ZB onto BluRay discs, then you'd have a stack of discs that can get you to the moon 23 times.*

> —David Reinsel (Senior VP of IDC)[2]

Example of Big Data based on size

For example, video as data can be large in nature since video is extremely rich and fairly difficult to compress, nor would we want to because the fidelity of video is what makes identification of objects in the video by AI vision more accurate, and *some* compression techniques *may* compromise quality.

For training purposes, we can use several long videos or many short videos for training purposes. Measured in minutes, more available video minutes will lead to better training. Also, pick videos that have activities in them. For example, a shorter video with many workers doing some construction activity is better than a long video of a tree in an empty park that has very few human activity.

Example of Big Data based on number of rows

Internet of Things (IoT) are major data sources today. IoT devices can be found everywhere in the commercial and consumer space. Think of the number of smart devices for homes that are readily available and pretty much plug and play.

---

[2]www.youtube.com/watch?v=eHTCR1BDhhA

Individually, data from IoT devices may not be large, but they make it up based on volume and velocity. Most IoT devices send status data on a regular basis and can provide thousands or millions of rows within a short span of time. Examples of the type of data IoT devices can send are

- The smart switches in a home

- GPS data used for navigation and routing

- IoT security systems and cameras

- Inventory information based on IoT tags

- Manufacturing and quality control IoT devices

Cisco Systems, a major provider of networking devices that power the Internet, stated in their 2018–2023 Annual Internet Report[3] that IoT devices will account for 50% of all global networked devices by 2023 (14.7 billion). Those IoT devices are expected to generate 5 quintillion bytes of data *per day*.[4] Gartner's[5] estimate for IoT devices are even higher, stating that in 2020, there will already be 20.4 billion IoT devices.

The "slight" discrepancy is really a nonissue because the bottom line is that there will be *a ton of data* that will fit our Big Data scenarios.

---

[3]www.cisco.com/c/en/us/solutions/collateral/executive-perspectives/annual-internet-report/white-paper-c11-741490.html

[4]https://blogs.cisco.com/datacenter/internet-of-things-iot-data-continues-to-explode-exponentially-who-is-using-that-data-and-how

[5]www.gartner.com/en/newsroom/press-releases/2017-02-07-gartner-says-8-billion-connected-things-will-be-in-use-in-2017-up-31-percent-from-2016

Today, more than 5 billion consumers interact with data every day—by 2025, that number will be 6 billion, or 75% of the world's population. In 2025, each connected person will have at least one data interaction every 18 seconds. Many of these interactions are because of the billions of IoT devices connected across the globe, which are expected to create over 90ZB of data in 2025.

—IDC and the Digitization of the World

Example of Big Data based on velocity

The volume of data can also be significant based on the velocity of the data. To illustrate velocity, a good use case is to look at the data generated by social media.

"Going viral" is the most popular phrase used to describe the velocity of information and news being transmitted through social media. In fact, *Forbes*[6] reported that at least 50% of Internet users get their news and information from social media. Furthermore, the average attention span of people consuming information is extremely short, so the information being spread on social media are in small chunks. This also means that many users of social media would generate, consume, and reshare that information in a high velocity. Twitter and the age of fake news is probably the most notorious case study. At a maximum of 280[7] characters a tweet, information is being tweeted and retweeted exponentially. Studies have also found fake information being transmitted at up to six times faster than real information.

---

[6]www.forbes.com/sites/nicolemartin1/2018/11/30/
 how-social-media-has-changed-how-we-consume-news/#38db7613c3ca
[7]At the time of writing.

Lastly, data from social media is generally richer than just plain text. For example, consider the content being shared on Instagram and Facebook. There may be titles and captioning, but for the most part, the information shared on these platforms are very rich. We will explore data trends in the next section, which best describes Big Data in the current context.

Other challenges of Big Data – data trends

When we use the term Big Data and where they are stored, we may have thought about relational databases like SQL Server, Oracle, or MySQL where the information are stored in tables with columns and indexes making up relational schemas. This is the traditional definition of data. This kind of data tends to be very structured with a predefined relational schema.

However, not all data today falls into columns with fields and indexes. In fact, most of the data in Big Data is not structured or relational. That is certainly the case with videos and photos, aside from the metadata of such content. But you cannot afford to not classify them as data. For example, take the case of security video footage or videos captured by law enforcement body cameras. These are all content that is being used in Line of Business (LoB) applications and sometimes in court for legal proceedings. Therefore, they are truly the new data types that need to be handled differently. We call this unstructured data.

Data also changes over time. Take a retailer, for example. Let us look at just one type of product that a retailer might sell, like a backpack. This simple product can easily fit in a structured database with fields like size, color, and weatherproof qualities or not. Then came along a change in trend that introduced a single strap backpack. Should the retailer add a field for number of straps or perhaps an indicator field for single strap and apply it to the entire table? Recently, there is also the trend for smart backpacks with charging capabilities for electronic devices. Then came along airport security (e.g., TSA friendly) backpacks. The bottom line is that new features and trends are introduced to products every time. So instead of adding new fields to the entire table that affects the entire product class, it may be better to have those fields present only when applicable. This is called semi-structured data.

There is also another better way to define certain data relationships rather than a traditional key-value pair in columns. For certain types of business cases, there are other data relationships and querying strategies that may be better suited than a traditional entity-relationship model. Consider this use case scenario – it is easier to map out relationships of data points by representing them as vertices and edges. This is widely used in social media to map the relationships between people. The database that manages this kind of data is known as a graph database.

You are probably no longer surprised you need more storage space than you purchased and continue to fall short. Not too long ago, it was gigabytes, but today, we are commonly referring to consumer-based storage in the terabyte range. That is because video takes up a lot of space. Your chat history with shared and reshared content is a space hog.

With the explosion of the amount and variety of semi-structured and unstructured data as well as high-velocity data, different approaches in storing, managing, and querying must be addressed.

Compute

Having access to Big Data is great for training models, but that can only be done if we have the equivalent compute to process and analyze the data.

To clarify, we use the term compute generally to represent the underlying infrastructure, which technically comprises the processor, memory, and storage.

Big Data's compute requirements are so large, we generally do not talk about it in terms of a single big and powerful computer, virtual or physical. But rather, we must rely on the ability to access clusters of big and powerful computers to work together to crunch the data. Consider what do these clusters translate to in terms of cost to operate and maintain if you were to build them yourself?

It has been estimated that to implement and maintain your own data warehouse and analytical infrastructure able to do machine learning and advanced analytics, you should be prepared to set aside a budget to cover a fully burdened cost[8] of $400,000–$500,000 per year.

We will explore this in greater detail in Chapter 7 where we cover Microsoft Databricks, a fully managed analytics platform.

Apache Spark and Hadoop

When we talk about Big Data, Apache Spark and Hadoop are almost always included in some context. This is because they are the most popular solution for analyzing Big Data.

Hadoop predates Spark, but both are open source solutions and leverage distributed computing to scale out processing of Big Data so analysis can happen in parallel, thus ensuring faster processing time than a compute infrastructure that can only scale up. Hadoop uses a Java-based algorithm called MapReduce to break the analysis into multiple smaller tasks and distribute them across all the computers that are in the cluster. The data is stored and in its own files system, called the Hadoop Distributed File System (HDFS), which is optimized to run on less expensive, consumer-grade hard drives (although it is highly recommended that your Hadoop architecture use enterprise-grade,

---

[8]Fully burdened cost takes into consideration all the costs associated with maintaining a compute environment, including personnel, environmentals, real estate square footage, and so on.

low-latency hardware like solid-state drives). The MapReduce algorithm can also experience latency in processing speed because MapReduce processes large datasets by splitting out the tasks and not the data. This can also be further limited to latency in data throughput (disk I/O).

Apache Spark addresses some of the shortcomings of Hadoop[9] by introducing in-memory processing, which boasts up to 100 times faster since disk I/O latency is removed from the equation. Another major difference between Spark and Hadoop as it relates to Big Data's data trend is the ability for Spark to handle streaming data. Streaming high-velocity data describes data that is continuously coming in as an input. For example, referring to our IoT use case scenarios, the type of data coming in from IoT devices are commonly streaming in nature. Hadoop is based on a batch-processing distributed file system model and therefore not suitable in handling streaming data. The ability to analyze streaming data enables real-time analysis and, therefore, triggering of real-time responses; this requires in-memory data structures and API libraries dedicated to streaming workloads. There are additional differences between Apache Spark and Hadoop, and it is beyond the context of this book to highlight all the differences, but these are the key concepts, similarities, and differences between Spark and Hadoop and how they handle Big Data challenges.

Note   Because Apache Spark is better suited for modern data trends, this book will focus primarily on Spark workloads. In Chapters and 7, we will start exploring the use of Azure Databricks, which is based on Spark. A good resource to get started on Spark and Databricks can be found at `https://docs.databricks.com/getting-started/spark/index.html`.

---

[9]Even though Hadoop has a distributed data processing architecture, it can still perform poorly for data writes and reads depending on the workload.

Apache Spark

As mentioned earlier, because Apache Spark is well suited to Big Data workloads, we would like to delve a little more into the Spark architecture in this section. Getting to better understand Spark is also a great precursor for our introduction to Azure Databricks in the following chapters.

When Big Data is distributed for processing, it uses a "driver and worker" model. The worker role, also known as the simple executor, is responsible for processing and analyzing its assigned portion of the dataset. The driver node acts as the coordinator that is responsible for distributing and tracking the workloads that have been assigned to the worker nodes. This relationship is being represented in Figure 6-2.

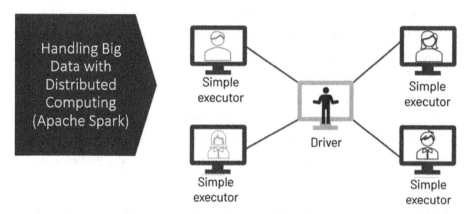

Figure 6-2. *Spark distributed compute*

Spark is comprised of a collection of libraries, APIs, and databases. There are three key Apache Spark interfaces – Resilient Distributed Dataset (RDD[10]), DataFrame, and Dataset. Of these three interfaces, you will work primarily with DataFrames and Datasets more than RDDs. We will explore the use of DataFrames and Datasets in Chapter 7.

---

[10]Reference – www.sciencedirect.com/topics/computer-science/
resilient-distributed-dataset

While this is a great approach to solving Big Data challenges, if an organization decides to build their own Spark environment, they will need to be prepared for the complexity and cost involved.

Aside from needing to provision, maintain, and support potentially different versions of Apache Spark, Linux, and the hardware, organizations that have deployed Spark often face memory and disk space optimization challenges, not to mention the need to update expensive hardware. There is also the need to have sufficient compute cores to use in the driver and worker roles. Furthermore, because a Spark cluster relies on different technologies and concepts, organizations need to have the skill set on at least the following technologies:

- Spark

- Linux

- Containerization

- Continuous Integrations/Continuous Deployment (CI/CD)

- Version control

- Logging and troubleshooting

- Hardware and memory optimization

- Job monitoring, control, and optimization

- Automation

- API libraries to load to satisfy particular workloads like streaming

Each of the earlier concepts and technologies usually depends on different open source solutions. Organizations should also be prepared to make in-house customizations to out-of-the-box open source packages. For a more in-depth appreciation of the complexity of managing your own on-premises Spark environment, listen to this presentation at Databricks'

Spark+AI Summit (starting from video marker 7'05") – `https://databricks.com/session/apache-spark-the-hard-way-challenges-with-building-an-on-prem-spark-analytics-platform-and-strategiesto-mitigate-this`.

At this point, we have articulated the benefits that Spark brings to the world of data science and machine learning. We have also discussed the complexity and cost of implementing and maintaining an on-premises Spark environment. The latter is the primary reason why Spark had been out of reach for many customers. There was a need to bring Spark's capabilities to the masses.

This is where Azure Databricks comes into the equation. Azure Databricks provides all the benefits of Spark without the management complexity and overhead and therefore makes advanced analytics of Big Data accessible to the masses.

Databricks

Databricks is popular in the data science and advanced analytics field because they provide a hosted Spark environment with the necessary tools for data engineers and data scientists, without the management overhead, complexity, and capital expense of hardware. Databricks is marketed as a Unified Analytics platform and is based on Spark.

All assets that are supported in traditional Spark, for example, Python libraries, Spark libraries, Jupyter notebooks, and ML libraries, are also supported in Databricks. Furthermore, Databricks extends the ability to implement source and version control for notebooks, support for collaboration between multiple data scientists, and support for different skill sets. For example, Databricks notebooks support SQL, Python, Scala, and R within the same notebook, thereby allowing data scientists who have different skill sets to easily collaborate.

In this section, we will explore Databricks (and Azure Databricks), Databricks concepts and services, and its applicability to different audiences. In Chapter 7, we will take these concepts and apply it in a more hands-on approach.

Azure Databricks

Azure Databricks is a specific implementation of the Databricks platform on Microsoft Azure. It is called a first-party partner solution, meaning that it is natively hosted within the Azure environment, shares the same network as other Azure resources, and has direct, fastest, and lowest-latency access to key resources generally required by Spark, such as compute clusters and storage. Finally, the management of the Azure Databricks environment is jointly undertaken by both Microsoft and Databricks engineers. Being a first-party partner application is the closest thing to a solution, whose Intellectual Property (IP) is not owned by Microsoft, can be in Azure.

One significant economic benefit of Azure Databricks aside from leveraging economies of scale of a public cloud is the ability to stop a cluster from running when not in use. This essentially pauses the hourly cost associated with the cluster and supports the "pay only for what you use" notion. Furthermore, the clusters can scale up and down when in use, and stopping the cluster is set to occur automatically in 120 minutes if there is inactivity, which can be configured as needed. We will explore this important feature in the next chapter.

Compared to an on-premises Spark cluster, once hardware is acquired, it is a sunk cost, and the only savings incurred from shutting down an on-premises cluster are power and environmentals. The per hour runtime cost of compute clusters in Azure Databricks is a fully loaded model which includes floor space, power, environmentals, physical security, hardware, monitoring, maintenance, and labor. These replace all the cost associated with having on-premises hardware. When taking the fully loaded cost into consideration, the savings are significant.

Aside from Azure Databricks, Microsoft Azure's intelligent cloud
initiative is comprised of multiple ML and advanced analytics solutions
such as Azure Data Factory, Azure Synapse Analytics, Azure Data Lake
Storage, Stream Analytics, and Azure Machine Learning Studio, just to
name a few of the commonly known services. Azure Databricks definitely
plays a significant role in the suite of solutions and is a core reason why
Microsoft Azure is ranked in the top right-hand quadrant of the Gartner
Magic Quadrant for Analytics and Business Intelligence in 2019. As seen in
Figure 6-3, not only is Microsoft Azure in the top right-hand quadrant, it is
significantly set apart from the rest of the competition.

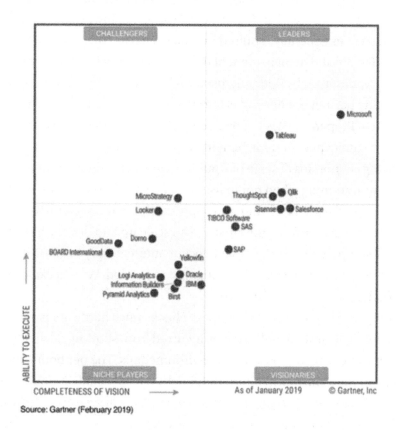

Figure 6-3. *Gartner Magic Quadrant for Analytics and Business
Intelligence (as of February 2019)*

Figure 6-4 also depicts the role Azure Databricks plays in the ecosystem of advanced analytics and business intelligence and where it lies in a modern data pipeline solution.

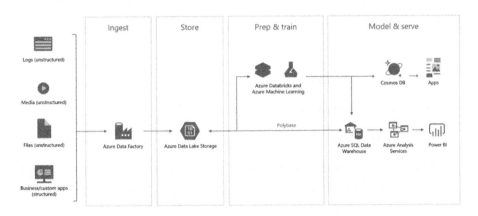

Figure 6-4. *Azure Databricks within Microsoft Azure's ecosystem of services catered to advanced analytics, BI, and ML[11]*

As seen in Figure 6-4, Azure Databricks is responsible for the "prep and train" phase of a modern data pipeline project. This means that Azure Databricks is a tool that caters two groups of audience – the data engineers and the data scientists. Azure SQL Data Warehouse has since been renamed Azure Synapse.

---

[11]Source: https://azure.microsoft.com/en-us/blog/azure-databricks-new-capabilities-at-lower-cost/v

Azure Databricks for data engineers

Around 90% of machine learning and analytics work is comprised of getting the data in the right "shape." What this means is that at a minimum, the data needs to be

- Complete
- In the correct format
- Fields correctly defined (schema)
- Clean

Completeness, format, correctly defined fields, and cleanliness of data are all interdependent and the primary responsibility of a data engineer.

Completeness

As mentioned earlier in this chapter, modern data comes from many different data sources and devices. Some are real time and others are not. In fact, one of the most challenging undertakings is to bring together the data from all the different disparate data sources. Data is considered complete when all the relevant data sources have been identified and the data from the sources can be successfully brought together. Traditionally, this is often accomplished through joins, merges, appends, inserts, and upserts. Making sure that there is an existing data pathway for the data to traverse is a key fundamental step. This step is commonly known as data ingestion, which we discussed in Chapter 3.

Correct format

Data may be collected and stored by the different devices and systems in a variety of formats. Some of the common formats are comma-delimited (csv) and tab-delimited (tsv) text files or files with fixed column locations. Data may also be collected in structured form like in SQL, MySQL, or

Oracle tables. Another modern data format is JavaScript Object Notation (JSON), which uses a nested flat file to represent potentially complex semi-structured data structures.

There may also be systems with proprietary data access (e.g., SaaS solutions) where there is no direct connection to the solution's database and may only be accessible via REST API calls, but such results are also often returned in JSON format.

Databricks itself uses a format called parquet files but supports almost all data formats. Being able to access all the data that exists in different formats, either natively or with the ability to use custom connectors, is key to bringing all the data together under the same roof before analysis can take place.

Proper schema

Schema includes field types, tables, and the relationships of the fields and tables to other fields and tables. Understanding the relationship schemas of fields from different tables (sources) would allow a data engineer to enrich a data source with more information which could become useful to the data scientist.

Aside from the relationships between fields and tables, a schema also defines the field type. Common field types include string, datetime, integer, and float, but there are others and more granular types. A field can also contain values that were calculated or derived from other fields. These are known as calculated fields and therefore depend on the accurate representation of the source fields involved in the calculation.

Data cleanliness

Data cleanliness describes the degree of which data can be used without causing errors or exceptions. It also includes de-duplication (dedup) of rows or gaps in time series data.

For example, if fields that are used as part of the mathematical operations that populate the values of calculated fields contain NULL values, this may cause inaccurate results. If fields contain unexpected or forbidden characters that are not handled, this may cause an error in the data analysis. For example, if a comma appears in an address field and that field is a csv file, the comma will be misinterpreted as the end of the field. Therefore, fields that may need such characters may need to be encapsulated by single or double quotes.

Data cleanliness can also be used to describe relevance. In some instances, fields that are not useful for data analysis can and should be removed to make the data model easier to understand and manage. For example, in the classic data science use case study of using the Titanic dataset, the fields containing the names of the passengers may not be useful to create a model to predict survivability, but the field describing the gender of the passenger is extremely relevant.

Extract, transform, load (ETL)

ETL is an acronym that pretty much sums up the responsibility of data engineers. It succinctly summarized the activities required to address the state of the data prior to handing it over to data scientists for analysis.

We covered the basics of data engineering in Chapter 3, but it is worth repeating it here again as a refresher or if you skipped that chapter. In recent years, a more modern variation of ETL has been proposed, and that is extract, load, transform (ELT). As its name implies, the transform and load steps have been reversed in this approach. In reality, ELT is a more accurate way of describing how tools like Azure Databricks, Azure Synapse Analytics, and Azure Machine Learning are used together with elastic storage like Azure Data Lake Store and Azure Blob.

Referring again to Figure 6-4, note that the data ingestion process is to pull together all the disparate data sources into a vast, highly elastic, and theoretically limitless storage solution, which in this case is Azure Data Lake Store (ADLS) and Azure Blob (see Chapter 3).

Tools such as Azure Databricks, Azure Synapse Analytics, and Azure Machine Learning are then optimized to access the data stored in ADLS or Blob. Most of the time, this is done via externally mounting the ADLS/Blob location onto the native Databricks File System (DBFS) or via Polybase external tables in Azure Synapse Analytics.

These techniques allow the data engineer or data scientist to immediately shape the data, remove fields, and combine fields on the fly. This flexible data representation is called schema on read and is a common approach for semi-structured data and data that is still being investigated for its value. Writing data to a fixed schema like in a relational data model is known as schema on write, where the schema is fixed and the business problem is well understood, so the flexibility is not as critical.

The transform step is also a less efficient and highly iterative process compared to loading. Different use cases and analysis requirements may also need different sets of data and fields. Thus, it makes more sense to expose all the available data and allow different groups of data scientists to consume only the data that is relevant to their analysis directly from ADLS/Blob.

Data that has been transformed appropriately for further analysis can then be stored in more traditional data warehouses, with connectivity back to ADLS/Blob to append new data, or refresh/upsert data as it changes. New incoming data can also be easily ingested through automation.

In Azure Databricks, one method is to transform and enrich the raw data in ADLS/Blob and then rewrite them back to ADLS/Blob as parquet files or store them directly with DBFS. Azure Databricks can also add an additional layer of technology, called Delta Lake, which allows you to analyze the changes in the data over the course of time. Delta Lake is beyond the scope of this book, but it is a recommended follow-up topic after you have mastered the concepts and topics from this book.

In summary, Azure Databricks can be an ELT tool for data engineers. In fact, Azure Databricks recently recognized that data engineering is a very big part of the data science workflow and, as such, introduced a new

219

tier of the Azure Databricks service known as Data Engineering Light.[12] This special tier of Azure Databricks recognizes that the ELT process does not need the power of distributed Spark for processing and analysis. Therefore, it is a tier that is optimized for ELT processes and, as such, costs less when Azure Databricks is used for such workloads.

Azure Databricks for data scientists

The main workload of a data scientist is to conduct experiments using statistical methods to analyze data. The goal is to develop a model that can accurately predict outcomes or mimic human intelligence. For example, models that can be used for scoring health outcomes for patients, or placing a traffic incident into a group that identifies likelihood of traffic signal failure, provide anomalies in the count of 911 call types in a time series.

These Databricks capabilities are foundational for the data scientist:

- Compute: An optimized and current Spark cluster

- Process: MLflow to manage the life cycle of model training, evaluation, and deployment

- Collaboration: Notebooks that support multiple users and multiple languages in order to maximize collaboration

- Extensibility: Support for industry leading open source ML frameworks like scikit-learn, PyTorch, and TensorFlow

---

[12]See https://azure.microsoft.com/en-us/blog/azure-databricks-new-capabilities-at-lower-cost/

Optimized Spark Engine

The key to optimizing ML involves technology, processes, and people. Earlier in this chapter, we have seen how Spark is the preferred technology to optimize the analysis of Big Data via distributed computing. With Azure Databricks, the people (data scientists) who carry out the experiments and analysis can provision, customize, and scale their Spark compute nodes. There are ways to limit the ability to carry out these functions, or create standards to govern such actions, but the goal is to empower data scientists to efficiently manage their own environment with minimal dependency on IT and infrastructure support professionals. We will see how compute is being deployed and customized in the next chapter.

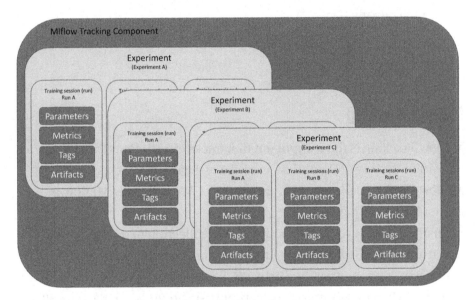

Figure 6-5. *MLflow Tracking and its role*

MLflow

The ML life cycle spans from data acquisition and preparation all the way to the deployment of an acceptable model. It is designed to be a continuous life cycle because new data will always be available and can therefore be used to improve the model.

The data acquisition and preparation portion of the ML life cycle have been discussed and presented as the domain of the data engineer. MLflow is an open source platform that manages and tracks the activities of the ML life cycle that are related to the experiments, training, development, validating, and continuous improvement of the ML models.

MLflow is made up of three primary components:

- Tracking
- Models
- Projects

MLflow Tracking

MLflow Tracking is the component that tracks experiments that are carried out within the Azure Databricks workspace. Figure 6-5 shows the role of MLflow Tracking as it relates to experiments. We will cover MLflow in greater detail in Chapter 8.

In the ML life cycle, an experiment is a collection of training sessions which are also called runs. For a run to occur, it would rely on certain parameters, tags, metrics, and artifacts. For example, recall from Chapter 2 where we looked at supervised learning using regression. We took 70% of the data for training and reserved 30% for testing purposes. This is an example of a parameter within a training session. During experimentation, we may pick different sets of data or different amount of data for training vs. testing purposes. Therefore, it is common for an experiment to have multiple training sessions, which with differently tweaked parameters.

Tracking and sharing the results from each run within the different experiments is the role of the MLflow Tracking component.

MLflow Models

The MLflow Model component allows us to manage and deploy models from a variety of ML libraries in any of our experiments, via the MLflow experiment user interface (UI). For example, we can load scikit-learn and train a model based on this framework. We can then deploy or share our scikit-learn trained model.

MLflow Projects

MLflow Projects is a method to organize code so that it can be easily shared and executed. It is based on a standardized format and set conventions that describe the code. The code can be stored in a directory or a GIT repo. Based on the standardized format and convention set forth by MLflow, other users or automated tools will know how to execute the code. Hence, MLflow Projects is important when it comes to automation in the ML life cycle.

Summary

In this chapter, we explored the reasons why distributed Spark is the best approach for handling Big Data, especially taking into consideration data trends. We also looked at the challenges and complexities involved with on-premises Spark environments, which is why machine learning was out of reach for so many organizations. Most importantly, we made the case for Azure Databricks as the ideal platform for data scientists because it provides all the benefits but removes all the barriers to entry, especially cost. In Chapter 7, we will focus on use cases and actual hands-on with Azure Databricks for both the data engineers and data scientists.

CHAPTER 7

Hands-on with Azure Databricks

In Chapter 6, we explored the concepts of Spark and Azure Databricks' implementation of the platform. In this chapter, we will be doing a hands-on exploration of these concepts in Azure Databricks.

Deploying Azure Databricks

Deploying Azure Databricks, like all other Azure services, is being done through the Azure portal at https://portal.azure.com (or https://portal.azure.us for Azure US Government[1]).

> **Note** Azure Databricks in Azure Government is a dedicated and separate implementation of Azure Databricks in the Azure Government cloud to meet US Federal Government regulatory requirements. Azure Databricks for Azure Government went into public preview on August 4, 2020.

---

[1] https://databricks.com/company/newsroom/press-releases/azure-databricks-now-available-on-microsoft-azure-government

© Julian Soh and Priyanshi Singh 2020
J. Soh and P. Singh, *Data Science Solutions on Azure*,
https://doi.org/10.1007/978-1-4842-6405-8_7

To complete the hands-on exercises in this chapter, you will need an Azure subscription. You can sign up for a free Azure subscription at `https://azure.microsoft.com/en-us/free/`. We will also make an assumption that you have a basic understanding of Azure and Azure concepts like resource groups. If you need to learn more about Azure, please refer to our other book, titled *Microsoft Azure, 2nd edition.*[2]

1. From the Azure portal, type "Databricks" (without quotes) in the search box at the top of the page.

2. Click Azure Databricks in the search results.

3. Click + Add.

4. Create a new resource group or select an existing one.

5. Provide a name for the Azure Databricks workspace.

6. For location, select a region closest to you.

7. For the pricing tier, select the 14-day trial (Premium) if it is available. Otherwise, pick the Premium tier.

Note   The Premium tier is required for role-based access control (RBAC). We need this to demonstrate collaboration through the use of Databricks notebooks in a later hands-on exercise.

---

8. Click Next: Networking >.

---

[2]`www.apress.com/us/book/9781484259573`

9. Keep the default option of not deploying the Databricks workspace to a vNet. This configuration is beyond the scope of this book. Deploying Azure Databricks to a vNet provides the added security of ensuring the environment is only accessible through private connections associated to your organization's corporate network like ExpressRoute or site-to-site VPNs.

10. Click Review + Create, and then click Create in the subsequent screen.

11. The deployment process will commence and will take a few minutes to complete. Once the Databricks workspace is deployed, click Go to resource. We will continue the hands-on exercise in the next section.

Exploring Azure Databricks

In this section, we will start exploring Azure Databricks. Getting familiar with the Azure Databricks UI is an important prerequisite prior to exploring its use for data engineering and data science.

1. Click Launch Workspace.

2. When launched, your workspace should look similar to what you see in Figure 7-1.

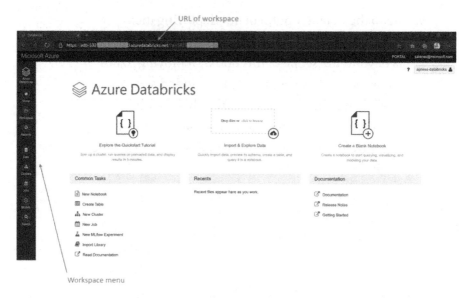

Figure 7-1. *Azure Databricks workspace*

3.   Referring to Figure 7-1 and comparing it to your workspace, note the URL. By bookmarking or using this URL, you can go directly to your workspace without going through the Azure portal to launch it. You can also share this URL with others so they can access this workspace, assuming that you have granted them the permission to do so (more on this later).

4.   To the left of the page, you will find the workspace menu, also shown in Figure 7-1.

Create Spark compute cluster

Look at the tasks listed under Common Tasks (also shown in Figure 7-1). As discussed in Chapter 6, the power of Spark is the ability to scale and distribute the analysis workload across multiple compute nodes. No analysis or actions (e.g., loading or refreshing data) can be done without a provisioned Spark compute cluster.

Therefore, one for the first task we need to do is to create and configure a compute cluster.

1. There are two ways to create a compute cluster. Either click New Cluster listed under Common Tasks, or select Clusters from the workspace menu. Go ahead and click "New Cluster" under Common Tasks.

Note   If we use the "New Cluster" option under Common Tasks, we will be presented with the screen to create a new cluster. If we choose Clusters from the workspace menu, we will see all the existing clusters, if any, and then by clicking Create Cluster, we will be routed to the screen to create a new cluster.

---

2. Provide a name for the cluster.

3. Hover over the question mark icon next to Cluster Mode, and read the description of the options. For this exercise, since you are likely going to be the primary user of this cluster to complete the exercises, select standard. For future reference, if we are creating a cluster that may be shared with multiple users doing different experiments at potentially the same time, choosing high concurrency as a shared cluster is the recommended option.

4. Like in step 3, hover over the question mark icon next to Pool, and read the description of the options. You will experience in a later step that it takes time to start a cluster. Therefore, if there is a sensitivity to delays in starting an experiment or job, we may want to reserve some minimum number of nodes to keep

in a running state to avoid spin-up delays. However, note that nodes that are running continue to incur compute cost. For this exercise, especially since no pools have been defined, select the only option of None for the pool.

5. Select the Databricks Runtime Version that best suits your needs. Each Runtime version has a description in parenthesis that describes the configuration. For example, for this exercise, we have selected Runtime 7.1 ML (Scala 2.12, Spark 3.0.0) because this configuration supports the hands-on exercise on Databricks-Connect later in the chapter, and it requires specific runtimes. This is an example as to why you would down version a configuration due to software dependency requirements. You may have to click Show More at the bottom of the drop-down box to see all the Runtime versions.

6. Uncheck and then recheck (toggle) the checkbox for Enable Autoscaling, and note the Min Workers and Max Workers options next to Worker Type. Checking the Autoscaling option provides us with the ability to specify the minimum and maximum limits of the number of workers. Remember in Chapter 6, we described how Spark distributes workloads among worker nodes and all the distributed workloads are being tracked and monitored by a driver node. For this exercise, keep Autoscaling checked and accept the default of 2 for Min Workers and 8 for Max Workers. This means that in subsequent exercises, as we use this cluster, there will always be a minimum of two worker nodes assigned.

7. In Chapter 6, we also discussed the benefit of clusters automatically terminating due to inactivity. This can significantly reduce cost and remove the management overhead of setting schedules to terminate unused clusters. With inactivity monitoring, cluster termination can occur dynamically. Not only is this a cost-saving mechanism, it is also a green initiative. Change the inactivity time-out from 120 minutes to 30 minutes.[3]

8. Now it is time to select the worker type. This is the actual *type* of compute resource that will be carrying out the work. The type and number of cores, and the amount of memory per compute node. The type of CPU can be a general CPU or one with a separate GPU to handle graphical or mathematically intensive operations (e.g., video analysis). Look through the available worker types in the drop-down list and note that you may need to click the "*x* more" options (where *x* indicates the number of additional option) at the bottom of each category. For this exercise, keep the default selection of Standard_DS3_v2. Cluster nodes have a single driver node and multiple worker nodes. The driver and worker nodes are usually the same type of compute instances (default) but may be different. As an example, we may choose to increase the memory of the driver node if we are planning to collect a lot of data from the Spark worker nodes to analyze them in the notebook.

---

[3]Optional exercise – what is the minimum and maximum number of minutes for the inactivity time-out?

Note   For detailed information on cluster configuration and the different cluster types, go to `https://docs.microsoft.com/en-us/azure/databricks/clusters/`.

---

9. Expand Advanced Options. We will not be making any changes, but if you need to customize the cluster, set environment variables, configure logging options, or run initialization scripts, this is where you will set these options. Click Spark, Tags, Logging, and Init Scripts tabs under Advanced Options to preview these settings.

10. Click Create Cluster at the top of the page. It will take a few minutes to create and start the cluster.

Customizing clusters

After the cluster is created, click it to change its configuration. The Databricks UI is intuitive and easy to navigate. One of the features we want to look at now is the ability to load custom libraries. This is a fairly common task. For example, we may want to use OpenCV for an object detection project in video feeds. To do so, we need to install the OpenVC library. Figures 7-2 and 7-3 show the the loading of the OpenCV_2.4.1 library in Java Archive (JAR) format. If you would like to use this JAR as a hands-on exercise to load into your cluster,[4] you can download it from this book's GitHub repo for this chapter at `https://github.com/singh-soh/AzureDataScience/tree/master/Chapter07`.

---

[4]Once loaded, the libraries will persist through shutdown and startup. Alternatively, initialization scripts at cluster config time can be used to load libraries.

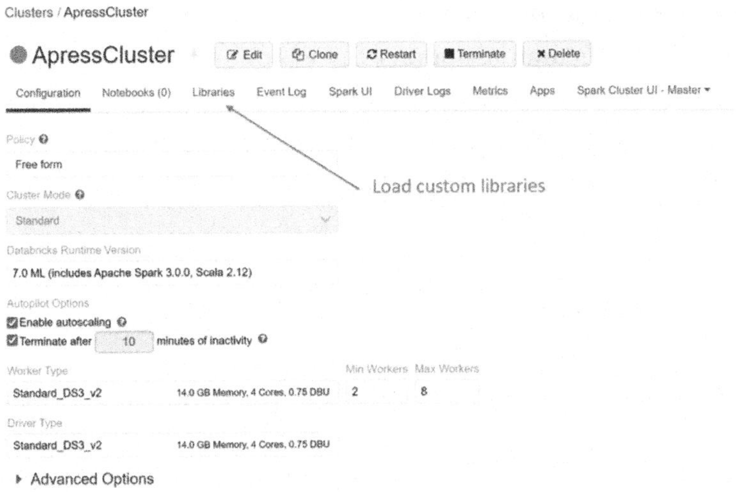

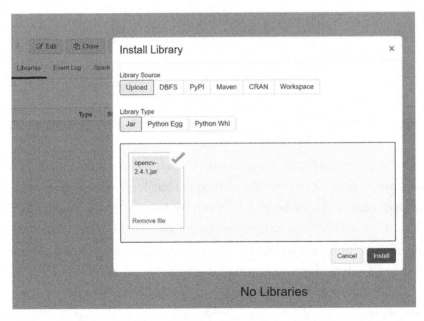

Figure 7-2. *Adding custom libraries to a cluster*

Figure 7-3. *Uploading and installing the OpenCV_2.4.1 JAR library*

Before leaving the topic on clusters and letting you explore the other cluster-related configuration options, there is one last important point we want to cover, and that is related to pinning.

Pinning a cluster can be done when a cluster is selected and the pin icon is selected, as shown in Figure 7-4.

Figure 7-4.   Pinning a cluster by clicking the pin icon

Pinning is important because it preserves the cluster if it is paused for an extended[5] amount of time. As mentioned earlier in this chapter, you can pause a cluster, or it may be terminated based on inactivity. When a cluster is paused, we will not be charged for the compute resources associated to the cluster. But when it is paused for an extended amount of time, the cluster itself will be deprovisioned and will no longer appear on the list of available clusters. Therefore, the cluster will need to be recreated, and if there were customizations associated with a deprovisioned cluster, like

---

[5]At the time of this writing, clusters that are paused for 30 days without being started will be deprovisioned.

the ones we discussed earlier, they will also be lost and will need to be reapplied to a newly created cluster.

Note   It does not cost anything to pin a cluster, and it is a good practice to pin a customized cluster, especially if it is extremely customized for specialized use cases. However, in the interest of making sure that compute resources can be dynamically reallocated, which is one of the core benefits of cloud computing, consider being selective on what should be pinned and what should not. Think of compute resources associated with pinned clusters as somewhat "reserved" and Azure intelligently manages such resources. During the COVID-19 pandemic, an unprecedented number of requests caused resource constraints, therefore causing some limitations and availability for certain types of compute resources. Even though Azure and cloud computing in general have large compute resource limits, the technical community should still be conscientious about resource utilization.

Connecting to clusters

There may times that you would need to connect to a Databricks cluster, usually for further configuration that can only be done by being directly connected.

One example scenario of this need is the installation of libraries that only uses *pip*. There are two methods to connect to a Databricks cluster:

- Using the Azure Databricks web terminal (preferred and easiest method)

- Using Databricks-Connect

> **Note**   While you can use Databricks-Connect to configure your
> cluster, the better scenario for using Databricks-Connect is to connect
> your favorite Integrated Development Environment (IDE) such as
> IntelliJ, Eclipse, PyCharm, RStudio, Visual Studio, and/or notebook
> server like Zeppelin or Jupyter to the Azure Databricks Spark cluster.
> If you only need to install a library, use the Web Terminal interface.

Azure Databricks web terminal

The easiest way to install packages and make further configuration
changes to your Azure Databricks cluster is to use the web terminal. But
before you can do this, you will need to enable the web terminal feature.

1. At the top right corner, click the user icon and select
   Admin Console, as shown in Figure 7-5.

Figure 7-5. *Accessing the Admin Console*

2. Select the Advanced tab, then scroll to the bottom of the list to locate Web Terminal, and then click the Enable button, as shown in Figure 7-6.

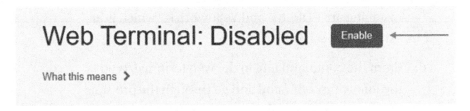

Figure 7-6. *Enabling the Web Terminal option*

3. Once the option is activated, refresh your browser.

4. Return to your cluster configuration page by clicking Clusters from the menu on the left, select the cluster, click the Apps tab, and finally click Launch Web Terminal, as shown in Figure 7-7.

Figure 7-7. *Launching the Web Terminal*

5. A separate browser window will launch, and you will see the terminal session. For this exercise, we will install two libraries that we will use in our notebook by using the *pip* command.[6] The libraries we will be installing are PDPbox[7] and Yellowbrick,[8] which is an extension of scikit-learn.

6. From the command line in the web terminal, type the following command and go through the prompts to complete the installation of PDPbox[9]:

```
pip install pdpbox
```

7. Do the same for yellowbrick[10]:

```
pip install yellowbrick
```

8. Figure 7-8 is a screenshot of both libraries successfully installed using *pip* via the web terminal.

---

[6]Pip is a package management system used to install and manage packages written in Python.

[7]https://pdpbox.readthedocs.io/en/latest/

[8]www.scikit-yb.org/en/latest/

[9]https://pdpbox.readthedocs.io/en/latest/

[10]www.scikit-yb.org/en/latest/quickstart.html

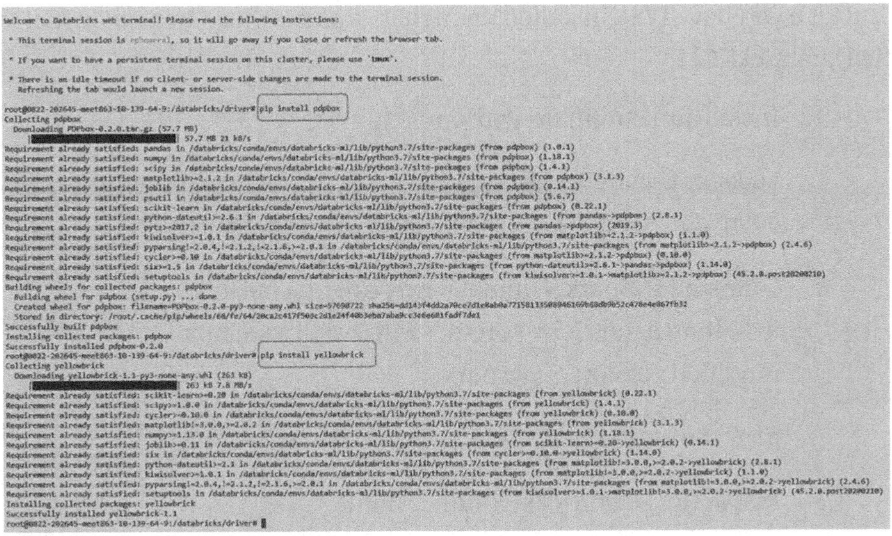

Figure 7-8. *Successful installation of PDPBox and Yellowbrick*

Databricks-connect

Databricks-connect is a Databricks Command Line Interface (CLI) that you install on a local machine that will then enable you to connect to a Databricks cluster from the local machine. The Databricks CLI can be installed on a Linux or Windows 10 machine.

The easiest way to install the Databricks CLI on a Windows machine is via the Windows Subsystem for Linux (WSL). WSL allows developers to run a Linux environment (Ubuntu distro) directly on Windows without the overhead of a traditional VM or the inconvenience of dual boot.

Detailed documentation and instructions on WSL can be located at https://docs.microsoft.com/en-us/windows/wsl/install-win10.

Once you have WSL installed, launch it, and use these steps to install the Databricks CLI:

1. Install and configure Python:

    ```
    sudo apt update && upgrade
    sudo apt install python3 python3-pip ipython3
    ```

2. Uninstall PySpark. Uninstall pyspark first because installing databricks-connect will install a slightly modified version of pyspark:

    ```
    pip3 uninstall pyspark
    ```

3. Install the Databricks-connect client:

    ```
    pip3 install -U databricks-connect==7.1
    ```

Note   Remember that when we created our Azure Databricks cluster at the beginning of this chapter, we selected Runtime 7.1ML. That is why we are installing version 7.1 of Databricks-Connect. The versions *must* match, including the minor version numbers, for example, pip install -U databricks-connect==6.6.

---

4. Select Cluster from the Databricks menu, and then select the cluster. Look at the URL of your Databricks workspace and gather the following information, as shown in Figure 7-9. We will need this information to configure Databricks-connect.

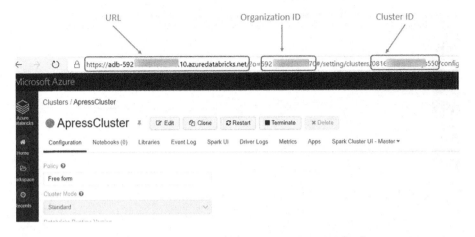

Figure 7-9. Getting the URL, Organization ID, and Cluster ID

5. Click the Edit button next to the cluster name, then expand the Advanced Options, and under the Spark tab, add the following two lines in Spark Config. This configures the cluster to listen on desired ports.

```
spark.databricks.service.port 8787 spark.
databricks.service.server.enabled true
```

6. Click Confirm and Restart. The cluster will restart.

7. Generate a user token by clicking the user icon on the right corner and selecting User Settings. Then click Generate New Token, as shown in Figure 7-10. The generated user token is used to authorize the use of Databricks REST APIs.[11]

---

[11]https://docs.databricks.com/dev-tools/api/latest/authentication.html

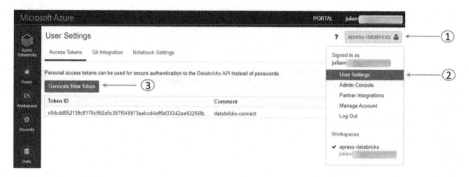

Figure 7-10. *Generating a user token*

Note   Take note of your token once it has been generated. Copy it somewhere that you can see and use it. Once you close the windows, you will not be able to see the token value any longer and will need to revoke and create a new one if you do not have the values stored somewhere. There is also a time to live (TTL) for the token (default = 90 days).

---

8. Go back to WSL and type:

    ```
    Databricks-connect configure
    ```

Note   If you get a warning that /home/<your_user_name>/.local/ bin is not in PATH, type PATH=$PATH:/home/<your_user_name>/. local/bin export PATH.

---

9. Accept the agreement and follow the prompts, providing the information you gathered in steps 4 and 7. Use port 8787 when prompted by the configuration, because that was what we configured it to be in step 5.

10. You can now test your connection to the Azure Databricks cluster, configure it, and connect your IDE or custom services to the Azure Databricks cluster. For more information on how to do this, please refer to `https://docs.microsoft.com/en-us/azure/databricks/dev-tools/databricks-connect`.

Note   If you ever forget your password on WSL, simply open a command prompt in Windows 10 as an administrator. Then type

Ubuntu config –default-user root

Relaunch WSL and use passwd username to reset the password of any user. Then use ubuntu-config –default-user username to reset future sessions back to your normal Linux user account. You can also reset or uninstall your WSL environment if needed. Go to Apps and Settings, select your WSL installation (search Ubuntu), click Advanced options, and then select Reset.

In conclusion, we have configured your Windows PC to connect directly to the Databricks cluster using the Databricks-Connect. Since this required a Linux VM, Databricks-Connect was not an easily available option for Windows users. By leveraging WSL v2, Windows users can now leverage Databricks-Connect and are not limited to just the Databricks workspace.

Databricks notebooks

Azure Databricks notebooks are very much like Jupyter notebooks that data scientists are familiar with. There is also the ability to integrate Jupyter notebook for local and remote workflows. See `https://databricks.com/blog/2019/12/03/jupyterlab-databricks-integration-bridge-local-and-remote-workflows.html`.

In this section, we will go through the creation and authoring of a notebook, as well as importing and exporting notebooks. We will also explore the collaborative capabilities of Azure Databricks so multiple data scientists and engineers can work off the same notebook.

Creating and authoring a notebook

In this first exercise, we will create a new notebook:

1. From the Azure Databricks menu, click Workspace, and then select Shared workspace, as shown in Figure 7-11.

2. Click the down arrow to expand the drop-down menu under Shared, and select Create, and finally select Notebook, as shown in Figure 7-11.

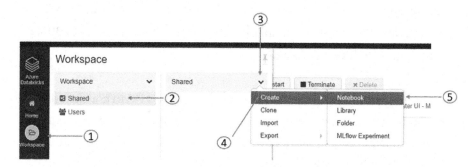

Figure 7-11. *Creating a new Azure Databricks notebook*

3. Give the notebook a name, and accept Python as the default language and the cluster that you have created earlier in this chapter. Click create.

4. The user interface of the Azure Databricks notebook should look familiar to anyone who has some experience with notebooks. There are cells for commands and controls located at the top right

244

corner of each cell to run, copy, cut, export, or delete a cell. The Azure Databricks notebook also uses the same shortcut keys (e.g., CTRL-Enter to execute a cell) and uses markdown language for text formatting.

5. We will go through a few steps to get familiar with editing a notebook. In the Cmd 1 cell, enter the following markdown:

```
%md
# This Notebook explores how a Data Scientist can carry
out statistical analysis on bank data
### (Banking data - Statistical applications)
```

6. Click anywhere outside the cell to exit from it. The formatted cell is now displayed.

7. However, close to the base of the first cell until the + icon appears, allowing you to insert a new cell, as shown in Figure 7-12.

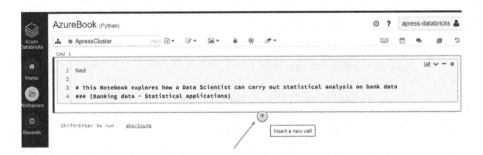

Figure 7-12. *Inserting a new cell*

8. Paste the following code into Cmd 2 cell. Take note of the lines where we are importing from the pdpbox and yellowbrick libraries that we installed earlier in the chapter when we configured the cluster.

```
#importing libraries
import numpy as np
import pandas as pd
import matplotlib.pyplot as plt
import seaborn as sns

from sklearn.preprocessing import StandardScaler
from sklearn.preprocessing import LabelEncoder

from sklearn.pipeline import make_pipeline
from sklearn.model_selection import
StratifiedShuffleSplit, StratifiedKFold
from sklearn.model_selection import cross_val_score
from sklearn.model_selection import GridSearchCV

from sklearn.linear_model import LogisticRegression
from sklearn.neighbors import KNeighborsClassifier
from sklearn.svm import SVC
from sklearn.ensemble import RandomForestClassifier
import xgboost as xgb

from sklearn.metrics import confusion_matrix,
classification_report

from pdpbox import pdp, get_dataset, info_plots

from yellowbrick.classifier import ROCAUC,
PrecisionRecallCurve, ClassificationReport
```

```
from yellowbrick.model_selection import
LearningCurve, ValidationCurve, learning_curve

import warnings
warnings.filterwarnings(action="ignore")
```

9. Hit CTRL+ENTER to run this cell.

10. In Chapter 3, we set up an Azure Blob Storage and
    used Azure Storage Explorer to upload the bank.
    csv dataset to the subfolder name datasets. Get the
    storage account name, access key, and container
    name. We will need it in the next step.

11. We will now access the bank.csv dataset in Azure
    Blob Storage that we uploaded as part of an exercise
    in Chapter 3. Add another cell, and enter the
    following code into Cmd 3 cell. Replace <your_
    Storage_Account_Name>, <container_name>,
    and <Your_Azure_SA_Access_key> with values
    from your lab (refer to Chapter 3 for a refresher if
    needed).

```
storage_account_name = "<your_Storage_
Account_Name>"
storage_account_access_key = "<Your_Azure_SA_Access_key>"

file_location = "wasbs://<container_name>@<storage_
account_name>.blob.core.windows.net/datasets/bank.csv"
file_type = "csv"
```

```
spark.conf.set(
    "fs.azure.account.key."+storage_account_name+
    ".blob.core.windows.net",
    storage_account_access_key)
```

12.   Press CTRL-Enter in Cmd 3 to execute the cell.

13.   Add a new cell and paste the following code to set
      up our dataframe:

```
df = spark.read.format(file_type).option
("inferSchema", "true").option("header","true").
load(file_location)
pdf = df.toPandas()
```

14.   Press CTRL-Enter in Cmd 4 to execute the cell.

15.   Expand Spark Jobs at the bottom of the cell, as
      shown in Figure 7-13 once the cell has been
      executed. Click the blue information icon to explore
      logging and diagnostic information for the nodes.

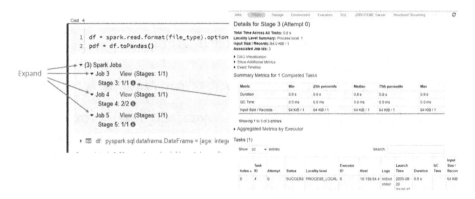

Figure 7-13. *Exploring information about Spark Jobs*

16. Next, as shown in Figure 7-14, expand dataframe, located beneath Spark Jobs, and look at the details of the dataframe and the schema that was inferred. Note the detected column names and data types.

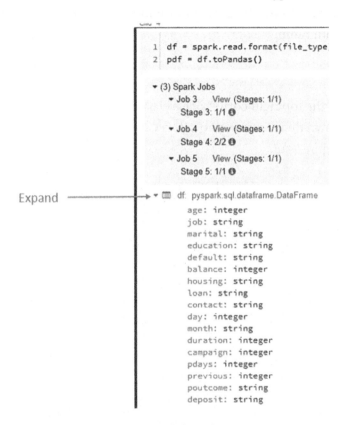

Figure 7-14. *Exploring the loaded dataframe*

17. Insert a new cell, and paste the following code. Press CTRL-Enter to execute the cell when done. This should give you a preview of the data in spark dataframe.

```
display(df)
```

18. Add a new cell, and enter the following code. Press CTRL-Enter to execute the cell when done. Since we created a pandas dataframe called pdf by converting the spark dataframe df in cell Cmd 4, we should be able to see the same information in a pandas dataframe.

    pdf

19. At the top right corner of Cmd 6 cell, click the down menu arrow, and select Cut Cell, as shown in Figure 7-15.

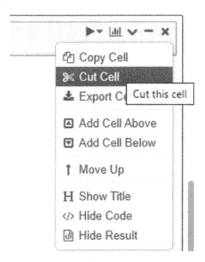

Figure 7-15. *Cutting a cell*

20. Hover between Cmd 4 and Cmd 5 and you should see an option to paste the cell, as shown in Figure 7-16. In this example, since we were planning to just move it up by one, we could have used the Move Up option instead of cutting and pasting the entire cell.

Cmd 6

```
1  display(df)
```

Paste cell here

▸ (1) Spark Jobs

age	job	marital	education	default	balance	housing	loan	contact	day
1	59	admin	married	secondary	no	2343	yes	no	unknown	5
2	56	admin	married	secondary	no	45	no	no	unknown	5
3	41	technician	married	secondary	no	1270	yes	no	unknown	5
4	55	services	married	secondary	no	2476	yes	no	unknown	5
5	54	admin	married	tertiary	no	184	no	no	unknown	5
6	42	management	single	tertiary	no	0	yes	yes	unknown	5
7	56	management	married	tertiary	no	830	yes	yes	unknown	6

Figure 7-16. *Inserting a cut cell*

21. Cmd 6 should now be the spark dataframe (not
    pandas). At the bottom of Cmd 6, there are options
    to change how the spark dataframe is being
    displayed. By default, it is in tabular form. Click the
    graph button, as shown in Figure 7-17.

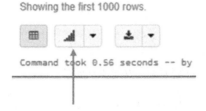

Figure 7-17. *Changing the tabular dataframe into a graph*

22. Use the options at the bottom of the cell to change
    the chart options and type and to resize the chart, as
    shown in Figure 7-18.

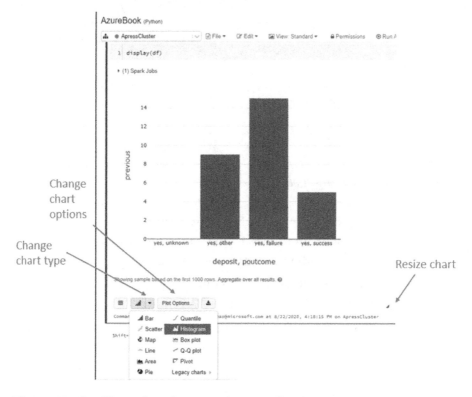

Figure 7-18. *Changing chart options and type*

We will leave you with the optional exercise of continuing to explore the graphical visualization capabilities of Azure Databricks notebooks.

Switching notebook default language

When we created the notebook, we selected the default language (Python). The default language of a notebook in Azure Databricks is always indicated next to the notebook's name in parenthesis, as shown in Figure 7-19. The default language is a hyperlink, and by clicking it, we get the option to change the default language for the notebook.

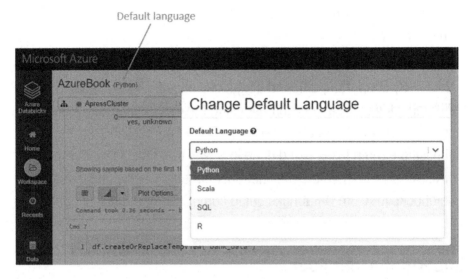

Figure 7-19. *Default language for a notebook and how to change it*

Setting a default language means that the syntax in any cell will be processed based on that language's interpreter unless the cell starts with a %md which would indicate to Azure Databricks to treat the contents as markdowns.

However, we can also start each cell with %sql, %r, or %scala, and Azure Databricks will treat the contents of that cell accordingly:

1. Add a new cell and paste the following code into the cell, and then execute it by using CTRL-Enter:

```
df.createOrReplaceTempView("bank_data")
```

2. Add another cell and paste the following code and execute it by using CTRL-Enter:

```
%sql
SELECT *
FROM bank_data
```

Notice that by using %sql, the notebook processes the simple select statement.

Note   By supporting different languages in cells, data scientists with different skill sets can collaborate using the syntax that they are most comfortable with. As a personal note, I have found myself picking and choosing certain tasks being done in a way that I feel is more efficient or comfortable. Therefore, it is not uncommon for even single user notebooks in Azure Databricks being comprised of multiple languages.

Importing a notebook

Now that we have a feel for authoring Azure Databricks notebooks, we will explore a more complete notebook by importing one from our GitHub repo.

1. Go to this book's GitHub repo and download the Bank Data Analysis notebook located at `https://github.com/singh-soh/AzureDataScience/tree/master/Chapter07/notebooks`. Notice the .dbc extension that indicates this is a Databricks notebook.

2. Select Workspaces from the Azure Databricks menu, select the Shared workspace, click the down arrow from Shared, and select Import.

3. Use the browse link or drag and drop the .dbc notebook file we downloaded from step 1 into the Import Notebooks dialog.

4. When the file is successfully read, the Import button will become available. Click Import.

We will explore more data science-specific concepts at our GitHub repo located at `https://github.com/singh-soh/AzureDataScience`. Such information can be updated and managed in a more frequent manner.

Note   We assume readers have some background in data science and ML or may have other sources from which to draw sample code and projects. Therefore, being able to efficiently use Azure Databricks to import sample notebooks, datasets, and projects is our focus in this chapter. Databricks provides a large repository of notebooks, and all the notebooks in Kaggle can also be imported to an Azure Databricks workspace.

Adding users

You can also add users to a workspace so they can collaborate with you. To add users

1.   Click the user icon located at the top right corner, and select Admin Console.

2.   Under the Users tabs, select Add User, and follow the prompt to add a user to the workspace.

3.   We can also create Groups in which we can then make users members of the groups and assign permissions at the group level.

4.   Lastly, note that for each user or group, you can prohibit or grant permission to create clusters.

Revision history

When collaborating with others, or even when you are actively working on a project by yourself, it is useful to be able to track the different versions of the notebook and be able to revert to a previous version.

Revision history is a built-in capability of Azure Databricks notebooks.

1. At the top right corner, beneath your user icon, click Revision history, as shown in Figure 7-20.

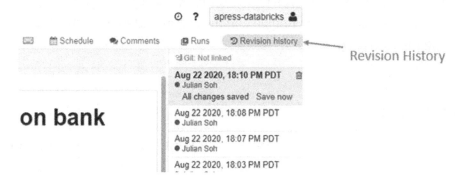

Figure 7-20. *Notebook revision history*

2. Pick any version, based on the date and time, and the snapshot of the notebook at that time will be displayed. If you want to permanently revert to a version, just click the Restore this version option.

Version control

Integrating version control for Azure Databricks notebooks is a best practice, especially if there are multiple collaborators. Notebooks contain code, experiments, and important data. Therefore, they should be treated with the same amount of sensitivity as traditional source code.

Azure Databricks can be integrated with Azure DevOps, GitHub, or Bitbucket. Instructions for integrating Azure Databricks with Git can be found at `https://docs.microsoft.com/en-us/azure/databricks/notebooks/azure-devops-services-version-control`. Once Azure Databricks is integrated with Git, we will see the sync status under Revision history as shown in Figure 7-21. Compare this to the Git status in Figure 7-20.

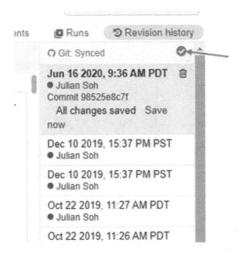

Figure 7-21. *Azure Databricks notebook integrated with Git for version control*

Summary

In this chapter, we were hands on with Azure Databricks and are now familiar with the fundamental concepts and UI. We covered the two core components of Azure Databricks – clusters and notebooks.

We also looked at data access from Azure Blob Storage. We will be sharing additional notebooks and code in our GitHub repo located at `https://github.com/singh-soh/AzureDataScience`.

In Chapter 8, we will look at ML and ML operations (MLOps) in Azure Databricks.

CHAPTER 8

Machine Learning Operations

Machine learning operations (MLOps) is DevOps for machine learning processes. MLOps enables data scientists to collaborate and increase the pace of delivery and quality of model development through monitoring, validation, and governance of machine learning models. This is equivalent to how DevOps helps software engineers develop, test, and deploy software quicker and with fewer defects. MLOps supports the data science life cycle just as DevOps supports the application development life cycle. As such, MLOps is based on the principles of DevOps.

Introducing MLOps

MLOps brings DevOps principles and concepts to machine learning, for example:

- Continuous Integration/Continuous Delivery (CI/CD)

- Source control

- Version control

- Testing

© Julian Soh and Priyanshi Singh 2020
J. Soh and P. Singh, *Data Science Solutions on Azure*,
https://doi.org/10.1007/978-1-4842-6405-8_8

Like DevOps, the goal of adopting MLOps is to promote more efficient experimentation that would lead to faster development and deployment of models. Source/version control and automated testing also promote quality assurance and security so models are not tempered in an unauthorized fashion. If you think about it, since models may be used to make decisions, potentially in life or death situations, they should be treated as mission critical assets.

Capabilities of MLOps

Azure machine learning provides the following MLOps capabilities.

Repeatable ML pipelines

ML pipelines define the steps for data preparation, training, and scoring processes. Depending on the data and the experiment, pipelines may be complex and require the steps to execute in a defined logic. ML pipelines are the backbone for all ML experiments. Once you have built a few pipelines that have been validated, the ability to repeat the process and reproduce similar pipelines, perhaps only with different datasets for example, is an efficient way to approach experimentation.

Reusable data scientist work environments

As mentioned in Chapter 1, a lot of work prior to experimentation is the preparation of the data scientists' work environment. This includes software that is needed for experimentation (e.g., Jupyter notebook), libraries catered to the type of data to be analyzed (e.g., PySpark, Keras for object detection, scikit-learn ML library), and the type and version of programming languages (e.g., Python, R, etc.).

It takes a lot of time to prepare the software environment, and due to features and compatibility, using the correct version of every component takes time to configure correctly. MLOps provide the capability to create reusable software environment that minimizes the need to reconfigure new environments.

Package, register, and deploy models

MLOps allows us to store and version our models in Azure within our ML workspace by registering the models in a model registry. This makes it easier for us to organize and track our trained models. Think of a registered model as a logical container that stores all the files that make up your model. For example, if we have a model that uses multiple datasets, multiple Python scripts, and several notebooks, these can all be registered as a single model in the Azure ML workspace. After registration, the model can be downloaded or deployed as a single action, and all the assets associated to the models will be handled as a single entity.

Registered models are identified by their names and versions. Every time a model with the same name is registered, the registry automatically increments the version number. MLOps also has the ability for us to use tags as additional metadata, which can facilitate search results.

Note   Azure MLOps can also be used to register models that are trained outside Azure Machine Learning.

Governance for the ML life cycle

The ML life cycle, akin to the Software Development Life Cycle (SDLC), consists of documentation, versioning, testing/scoring results, requirements, and so on. It is essentially all the information pertaining to an ML project and affects all the assets tied to the project.

Azure ML provides the ability to track and provide an end-to-end audit trail for all our ML assets. This is done by

- Leveraging Git integration and using repos, branching, and commits to track code.

- Providing a capability known as Azure ML Datasets to track, profile, and version datasets.

- Providing a feature called Azure ML Model Interpretability which captures metadata that describes models, meets regulatory compliance, and explains the logic between input data and results. Recalling our discussion around ethical AI, this feature is an example of Microsoft Azure ML committing to that initiative.

- Tracking run history: Azure ML run history stores a snapshot of the code, data, and computes used to train a model at every iteration of the training cycle.

- Deployment of models: Once a model has been developed, debugged, and ready for deployment, it can be packaged into a docker image. Models can be deployed as web services in the cloud or locally and, as such, can be deployed at the edge like an IoT device.

Note   During deployment, we have the option to convert a model to Open Neural Network Exchange (ONNX). ONNX is an optimized format that could provide up to 2x in performance improvement. Software services that support ONNX increase the opportunity for reuse and interoperability across disparate ML systems. For example,

Azure Synapse SQL Pools supports ONNX, allowing TSQL queries to PREDICT() outcomes for a SQL dataset. Optimizing models is beyond the scope of this book, but there are extensive resources dedicated to this topic, and it is also a very important step in model development.

- Automation: A key component of governing the ML life cycle is automation. Changes in models, like in software, should be rolled out in a controlled but timely fashion, with minimal need for manual intervention. This process is known as Continuous Integration/ Continuous Deployment (CI/CD). Azure MLOps achieves this by leveraging its integration with Azure DevOps.

Azure ML pipelines hands-on

Azure ML pipelines were introduced in Chapter 4 of this book, and in this chapter, we will build pipelines on bank marketing dataset to operationalize our workload. Azure ML pipelines stitch together multiple phases of ML cycle to be executed independently after users move beyond exploratory analysis and into iterative process of model training, deploying, and operationalizing. With huge amount of data and model training, there comes an additional responsibility of streamlining accessibility to development phase and reusability of complex workflows. However, majority of organizations are deploying machine learning applications without proper structure, governance, and reproducible code in place which leads to inefficient delivery and time spent on gathering metrics, model versions, hyperparameters, and managing this environment, and lastly it becomes a never-ending battle to rebuild or iterate the processes.

Azure ML pipelines address these operational challenges and provide users with great benefits to build the ML application foundation strong so it's easier to manage every time there are changes in data, models, parameters, team members, or in dealing with fault tolerance. Azure ML pipelines optimize your workloads for simplicity, speed, repeatability, versioning and tracking, quality assurance, cost control, scaling, and distributed computing to build efficient and easily manageable applications.

As discussed earlier, machine learning workflow can be broken down into multiple steps, and with Azure ML pipelines, users can run/track distinct steps and tweak only the steps required to be reconfigured without impacting other steps in the pipeline. For example, once the pipeline is designed, often training step requires more fine-tuning to improve model performance, so when the pipelines are rerun, the execution would jump to update training script step without having to run other steps where code hasn't changed at all. This approach saves data scientist time allowing them to focus on building ML model rather than handling infrastructure. Distinct steps also make it easy to use different compute targets/clusters of different sizes at each step. Some of the major Azure ML pipeline features are discussed as follows:

1. Unattended execution (scheduled scripts)

2. Mixed and diverse compute

3. Reusability

4. Tracking and versioning

5. Collaboration

6. Modularity (isolated changes)

Azure ML pipelines have pre-built steps/modules to cover many common scenarios used in machine learning like data_transfer_step, automl_step, python_script_step, parallel run step, and so on. To read more on each step, refer to this link: `https://docs.microsoft.com/en-us/python/api/azureml-pipeline-steps/azureml.pipeline.steps?view=azure-ml-py`:

Next we will build the pipeline for bank marketing data to prep and train the model. This hands-on exercise is to get you started with Azure ML pipelines and configure steps. There are a variety of scenarios Azure ML pipelines can be used, and I encourage readers to practice steps (not covered in this chapter) and build MLOPs environment for their project.

Hands-on lab with Azure ML pipelines:

It's important to finish the hands-on lab of Chapter 5 before starting this lab. The concepts and code will be better understood, and users will be able to run the code successfully.

If you're doing this hands-on lab directly, make sure to at least complete the prerequisite setup in Chapter 5, and run the commented out code in notebook BankMarketing_Pipelines.ipynb. We will follow this process to build a pipeline:

1. Set up machine learning libraries/resources.

2. Set up a compute target.

3. Configure a training run's experiment.

4. Set up Datastore, and configure Dataset (done in Chapter 5).

5. Construct pipeline steps.

We will use Azure ML compute instance (configured in Chapter 5) to use JupyterLab to reduce the environment setup issues. To configure compute instance, please refer to "Getting Started with JupyterLab" section of Chapter 5. Once you're in JupyterLab, git clone the following GitHub folder. The ML pipeline folder is all set up, and to get started, just launch the BankMarketing_Pipelines.ipynb notebook.

https://github.com/singh-soh/AzureDataScience/tree/master/Chapter08_MLOPS/ML_Pipelines.

1. **Set up machine learning libraries.** Run first cell to import all the necessary packages (Figure 8-1).

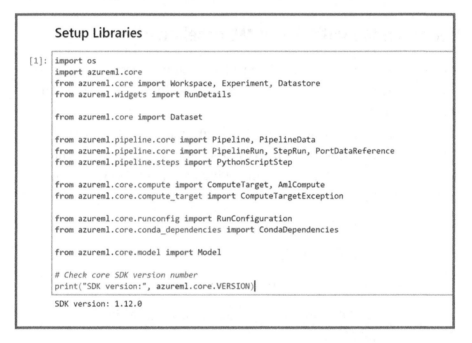

Figure 8-1. *Install Azure ML libraries in Python SDK*

2. Initialize workspace and create or use existing compute target (Figure 8-2).

Initialize AzureML Workspace

```
[2]: ws = Workspace.from_config()
```

Create Comput Target or use existing one

```
[4]: from azureml.core.compute import ComputeTarget, AmlCompute
     from azureml.core.compute_target import ComputeTargetException

     # Choose a name for your CPU cluster
     aml_compute = "automatecluster"

     # Verify that cluster does not exist already
     try:
         aml_compute = ComputeTarget(workspace=ws, name=aml_compute)
         print('Found existing cluster, use it.')
     except ComputeTargetException:
         compute_config = AmlCompute.provisioning_configuration(vm_size='STANDARD_D2_V2',
                                                                max_nodes=4)
         aml_compute = ComputeTarget.create(ws, aml_compute, compute_config)

     aml_compute.wait_for_completion(show_output=True)

     Found existing cluster, use it.
     Succeeded
     AmlCompute wait for completion finished

     Minimum number of nodes requested have been provisioned
```

Figure 8-2. *Create compute target in Python SDK*

3. Configure training run's experiment (Figure 8-3).
   This provides training run to have all the software
   dependencies needed by training steps. Users
   have the flexibility to use curated or pre-baked
   environment with common interdependent
   libraries which is faster to bring online. We will use
   custom-defined environment; in this case, a new
   docker image will be created and registered in Azure
   container registry. Run the next cell to create the
   environment.

Configure the training run's environment

```
[37]: from azureml.core.runconfig import RunConfiguration
      from azureml.core.conda_dependencies import CondaDependencies

      # Create a new runconfig object
      aml_run_config = RunConfiguration()

      # Use the aml_compute you created above.
      aml_run_config.target = aml_compute

      # Enable Docker
      aml_run_config.environment.docker.enabled = True

      # Set Docker base image to the default CPU-based image
      aml_run_config.environment.docker.base_image = "mcr.microsoft.com/azureml/base:0.2.1"

      # Use conda_dependencies.yml to create a conda environment in the Docker image for execution
      aml_run_config.environment.python.user_managed_dependencies = False

      # Specify CondaDependencies obj, add necessary packages
      aml_run_config.environment.python.conda_dependencies = CondaDependencies.create(
          conda_packages=['pandas','scikit-learn'],
          pip_packages=['azureml-dataset-runtime[fuse]', 'packaging', 'numpy==1.16.2','azureml-sdk'])

      print ("Run configuration created.")

      Run configuration created.
```

Figure 8-3. *Create run configuration in Python SDK*

4. Set up Datastore, and configure Dataset (Figure 8-4). We have configured Datastore and Datasets in Chapter 5 lab. The commented out code is for reference as those were all achieved in Chapter 5.

Configure Datasets and Datastore

```
[ ]: # ### Upload data to datastore and register datasets.
     # from azureml.core import Datastore
     # blob_datastore_name='kaggledatabook' # Name of the datastore to workspace
     # container_name=os.getenv("BLOB_CONTAINER", "opendata") # Name of Azure blob container
     # account_name=os.getenv("BLOB_ACCOUNTNAME", "kaggledatabook") # Storage account name
     # account_key=os.getenv("BLOB_ACCOUNT_KEY", "QGmWeGNpXKFtmU7cnXW5Dg0LwX7L2SCbfjs2iBKXHigsdhABgTfFoSVh4ja3KTFdCfDrh7Q6n3SGpVLE4g/eXA==

     # blob_datastore = Datastore.register_azure_blob_container(workspace=ws,
     #                                                          datastore_name=blob_datastore_name,
     #                                                          container_name=container_name,
     #                                                          account_name=account_name,
     #                                                          account_key=account_key)

     # blob_datastore.upload_files(files = ['./Bank.csv'], overwrite = True, show_progress = True)
     # from azureml.core.dataset import Dataset
     # bank_dataset = Dataset.Tabular.from_delimited_files(path=blob_datastore.path('Bank.csv'))
     # bank_dataset

[38]: blob_datastore = Datastore.get(ws, "kaggledatabook")

[82]: from azureml.core.dataset import Dataset
      bank_dataset = Dataset.get_by_name(ws, name='bank_dataset')
```

Figure 8-4. *Set up Datastore and Datasets in Python SDK*

5. Construct your pipeline steps (Figure 8-5). Once
    everything is defined and environment is created,
    we are ready to create our pipeline steps.

Construct your pipeline steps

```
[76]: from azureml.pipeline.core import PipelineData
      from azureml.pipeline.steps import PythonScriptStep

      # python scripts folder
      prepare_data_folder = './scripts/prepdata'

      # Define output after cleansing step
      cleansed_data = PipelineData("cleansed_data", datastore=blob_datastore).as_dataset()

      print('Cleanse script is in {}.'.format(os.path.realpath(prepare_data_folder)))

      # cleansing step creation
      # See the cleanse.py for details about input and output
      cleansingStep = PythonScriptStep(
          name="Cleanse Bank Marketing Data",
          script_name="prep.py",
          arguments=["--output_cleanse", cleansed_data],
          inputs=[bank_dataset.as_named_input('bank_dataset')],
          outputs=[cleansed_data],
          compute_target=aml_compute,
          runconfig=aml_run_config,
          source_directory=prepare_data_folder,
          allow_reuse=True
      )

      print("cleansingStep created.")
```

```
Cleanse script is in /mnt/batch/tasks/shared/LS_root/mounts/clusters/adscompute/code/Users/prsing/Bank
scripts/prepdata.
cleansingStep created.
```

Figure 8-5. *Construct data prep pipeline step in Python SDK*

- A typical initial pipeline step includes dataprep
  step (prep.py) which is put in a subdirectory/source
  directory which gets uploaded to the compute target
  as part of the pipeline creation process. In our case, it's
  prepare_data_folder.

- The step runs the script specified in script_name with
  arguments and input and output values specified in the
  step.

269

- Arguments are passed to be used in prep.py script.

- The input dataset can be referenced using as_named_
  input (<name of dataset in AMLworkspace>) in
  download or mount mode.

- Intermediate data or output of a step is represented
  using PipelineData objects which creates a data
  dependency between steps and hence creates
  execution order of steps in a pipeline. In our scenario,
  cleansed_data is the produced output of data prep step
  and can be used as input in one or more steps.

- This particular step will be run on machine defined by
  compute_target and will use the configuration defined
  in runconfig.

- Pipeline's key feature is to use "allow_reuse". This is the
  default behavior of the step as long as script_name,
  inputs, and parameters of step remain the same. Setting
  "allow_reuse" to True lets you use the results from
  previous run and immediately moves to the next step.
  This behavior saves huge amount of time as long as the
  changes are made in training step; this capability will
  run the pipeline without running or creating a new run
  for previous steps. If allow_reuse is set to False, a new
  run will be generated every time pipeline is executed.

Your prep.py should look like Figure 8-6 with Run object, arguments, and output defined. We are using the same cleaning code used in Chapter 5 hands-on; here, we are wrapping with pipeline objects to operationalize and log times to run this step.

```
print("Cleans the input data")
run = Run.get_context()
# get input dataset by name
run.log("data cleaning start time", str(datetime.datetime.now()))
bank_dataset = run.input_datasets['bank_dataset']

parser = argparse.ArgumentParser("prep")
parser.add_argument("--output_cleanse", type=str, help="cleaned and transformed bank marketing data directory")
args = parser.parse_args()
print("Argument (output cleansed bank marketing data path): %s" % args.output_cleanse)

#to pandas dataframe
data = bank_dataset.to_pandas_dataframe()

# Data Cleaning
cat_col = ['default', 'housing', 'loan', 'deposit', 'job',
           'marital', 'education', 'contact', 'month', 'poutcome']
for column in cat_col:
    label_encoder = LabelEncoder()
    label_encoder = label_encoder.fit(data[column])
    label_encoded_y = label_encoder.transform(data[column])
    data[column + '_cat'] = label_encoded_y
data = data.drop(columns = cat_col)

#drop irrelevant columns
data = data.drop(columns = ['pdays'])
#impute incorrect values and drop original columns
def get_correct_values(row, column_name, threshold, df):
    ''' Returns mean value if value in column_name is above threshold'''
    if row[column_name] <= threshold:
        return row[column_name]
    else:
        mean = df[df[column_name] <= threshold][column_name].mean()
        return mean
data['campaign_cleaned'] = data.apply(lambda row: get_correct_values(row, 'campaign', 50, data),axis=1)
data['previous_cleaned'] = data.apply(lambda row: get_correct_values(row, 'previous', 50, data),axis=1)
data = data.drop(columns = ['campaign', 'previous'])

if not (args.output_cleanse is None):
    os.makedirs(args.output_cleanse, exist_ok=True)
    print("%s created" % args.output_cleanse)
    path = args.output_cleanse + "/processed.parquet"
    write_df = data.to_parquet(path)
run.log("data cleaning end time", str(datetime.datetime.now()))
```

Figure 8-6. *Prepare Prep.py script for data prep step*

Next we will create train model step (Figure 8-7). We will pass all the necessary information the same way we passed in the previous step with arguments being hyperparameters for gradient boosting model and a model argument for the output.

```
model_file = PipelineData("model_file", datastore=blob_datastore)

train_model_folder = './scripts/trainmodel'
trainmodel = PythonScriptStep(name="train_step",
                    script_name="./train.py",
                    arguments=['--learning_rate', 0.01,
                                '--n_estimators', 600,
                                '--max_depth', 9,
                                '--min_samples_split', 1200,
                                '--min_samples_leaf', 60,
                                '--subsample', 0.85,
                                '--random_state', 10,
                                '--max_features', 7,
                                '--model',model_file],
                    inputs= [cleansed_data.parse_parquet_files(file_extension=None)],
                    outputs=[model_file],
                    compute_target=aml_compute,
                    runconfig=aml_run_config,
                    source_directory=train_model_folder,
                    allow_reuse=True)
```

Figure 8-7. *Construct train model pipeline step in Python SDK*

For the purpose of this book, we have used only two steps to
demonstrate building pipeline with steps; there could be more steps
added in practice. For example, data preparation phase can further be
built in multiple steps – clean data, transform data, normalize data, feature
engineer data, and so on. Figure 8-8 shows one way of building steps for
each of the phases.

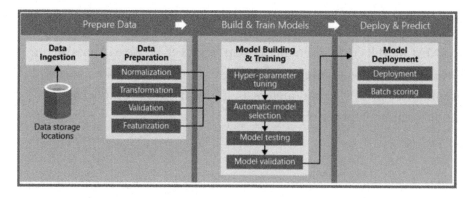

Figure 8-8. *Machine learning process break-down in multiple steps.
Source: https://github.com/Azure/MachineLearningNotebooks/
tree/master/how-to-use-azureml/machine-learning-pipelines*

So now we have created train model step; let's look into train.py script. The training script in Figure 8-9 takes input data from PipelineData object created in the previous step for output. We split the data in training and testing and train gradient boosting model to predict term deposit by the client. After the model is created, we are also registering the mode in Azure ML model registry. Users can also create a separate step for model register to separate the process from training and improve speed as well as efficiency.

```
run = Run.get_context()
clean_data = run.input_datasets['cleansed_data']
# get input dataset by name
data = clean_data.to_pandas_dataframe()
run.log("Training start time", str(datetime.datetime.now()))

# Model Training
X = data.drop(columns = 'deposit_cat')
y = data[['deposit_cat']]

X_train, X_test, y_train, y_test = train_test_split(X, y, test_size = 0.15, random_state = 300)

Params = {'learning_rate': np.float(args.learning_rate),
          'n_estimators': np.int(args.n_estimators),
          'max_depth': np.int(args.max_depth),
          'min_samples_split': np.int(args.min_samples_split),
          'min_samples_leaf': np.int(args.min_samples_leaf),
          'subsample': np.float(args.subsample),
          'random_state': np.int(args.random_state),
          'max_features': np.int(args.max_features)}

# GradientBoostingClassifier
model = GradientBoostingClassifier(**Params)
model.fit(X_train,y_train.squeeze().values)

#calculate and print scores for the model
y_train_preds = model.predict(X_train)
y_test_preds = model.predict(X_test)

model_file_name = 'joblibGB_bankmarketing.sav'

accuracy_score_train = accuracy_score(y_train, y_train_preds)
accuracy_score_test = accuracy_score(y_test, y_test_preds)
run.log('Gradient Boosting Accuracy Score for training', accuracy_score_train)
run.log('Graident Boosting Accuracy Score for testing', accuracy_score_test)

# Save the trained model
os.makedirs('outputs', exist_ok=True)
joblib.dump(value=model, filename='outputs/' + model_file_name)

run.upload_file("outputs/joblibGB_bankmarketing.sav", "outputs/joblibGB_bankmarketing.sav")
model = run.register_model(model_name = 'bankmarketing_GBmodel_pipeline', model_path = 'outputs/joblibGB_bankmarketing.sav')
run.log("Training end time", str(datetime.datetime.now()))
run.complete()
```

Figure 8-9. *Prepare train.py script for training model step*

Now that we have built the steps and scripts that go in those steps, we will combine the steps in pipeline object and submit the execution (Figure 8-10). Pipelines are submitted using Experiment class which track multiple pipeline runs under the same experiment name.

```
         Combine steps and submit the pipeline

[79]:    steps = [cleansingStep,trainmodel]

[80]:    pipeline1 = Pipeline(workspace=ws, steps=steps)

[81]:    pipeline_run1 = Experiment(ws, 'Bank_Marketing').submit(pipeline1, regenerate_outputs=False)

         Created step Cleanse Bank Marketing Data [5d082efb][091249ef-40a6-4d2e-a29f-79c3d68a49ac], (This step is eligib
         run's output)
         Created step train_step [f4cb3f05][03c8531d-4a30-46c1-8a16-de577be0a842], (This step will run and generate new
         Submitted PipelineRun 62f1d8fb-feb3-4824-bceb-3ff7d24cbad7
         Link to Azure Machine Learning Portal: https://ml.azure.com/experiments/Bank_Marketing/runs/62f1d8fb-feb3-4824-
         =/subscriptions/ab8f5415-63b3-4fd4-8a8a-9213316abb6e/resourcegroups/ADS_Book/workspaces/ADS_AMLworkspace
```

Figure 8-10. *Combine pipeline steps and submit Experiment*

Once the experiment is submitted, click the link provided to track it on Azure ML workspace portal as well.

Once completed, you will be able to see the graph view of pipeline and each step logged metrics (Figure 8-11).

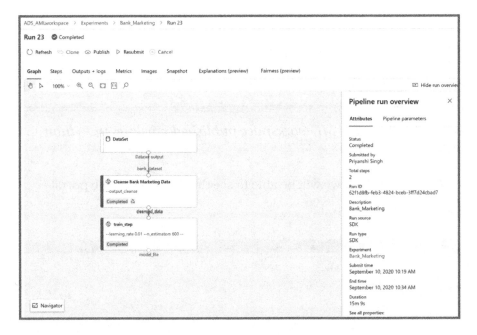

Figure 8-11. *Azure ML workspace pipeline run on portal*

Publishing and tracking machine learning pipelines

Machine learning pipelines are a great way to introduce reproducibility
and reusability in machine learning workloads. Pipeline versioning
increases collaboration among team members and lets users develop
newer pipelines or steps to embed in existing one. Publishing a pipeline
lets users deploy a pipeline as a rest endpoint so it can be invoked with
different inputs and from any external systems including non-Python
applications. This endpoint can be used for batch scoring as well in
conjunction with other Azure services. So now we tested our pipeline, and
it runs successfully. Let's go ahead and publish it to create a rest endpoint.
Note: Pipelines can also be published from portal.

Run the next cell to publish the pipeline as shown in Figure 8-12.

```
       Publishing the pipeline

[87]:  published_pipeline1 = pipeline_run1.publish_pipeline(
           name="BankMarketing_GB_Pipeline",
           description="Predict Term Deposit pipeline on bank marketing dataset",
           version="1.0")
```

Figure 8-12. *Azure ML workspace published pipelines in Python SDK*

Once published, we will be able to see the endpoint on the portal (Figure 8-13).

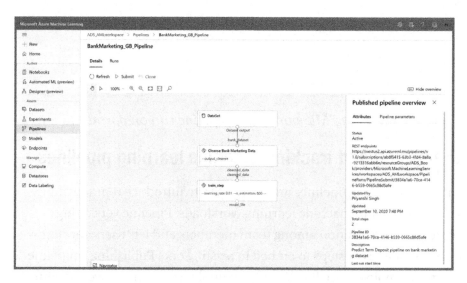

Figure 8-13. *Azure ML workspace published pipeline with rest endpoint*

Now that it exists as a rest endpoint, we can schedule the pipelines and track runs. Pipelines can be scheduled in two ways: time-based schedule and change-based schedule. Time-based schedule is good for routine tasks, for example, generating forecast every hour or month. Change-based schedules are good to trigger the pipeline based on an event, for example, new data added or data changes. So let's go ahead and create a time-based schedule for our pipeline runs with 5 minute frequency (Figure 8-14).

```
Schedule a pipeline

[91]:  from azureml.pipeline.core.schedule import ScheduleRecurrence, Schedule

       recurrence = ScheduleRecurrence(frequency="Minute", interval=5)
       recurring_schedule = Schedule.create(ws, name="bankmarketing_recurring5min",
                                description="Based on time",
                                pipeline_id="3834a1a6-70ca-4146-b559-0665c88d5afe",
                                experiment_name="Bank_Marketing",
                                recurrence=recurrence)
```

Figure 8-14. *Azure ML workspace pipeline schedule in Python SDK*

Once the schedule is created, we can track pipeline execution every 5 minutes and set up rules in terms of failure. Users can be alerted via email or message if the pipeline fails. Azure ML workspace will be tracking your pipeline runs, and we should be able to see on the portal (Figure 8-15).

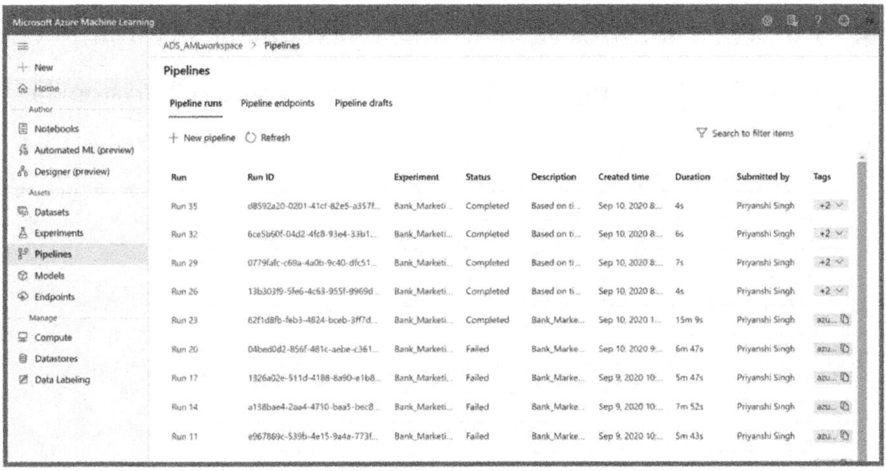

Figure 8-15. *Azure ML workspace pipeline runs every 5 minutes*

You would notice that time taken to run the complete pipeline is significantly less in consecutive runs as it's using allow_reuse as True which is enabling the pipeline steps to use the results from the previous runs as long as script name, input data, and parameters remain the same for the steps. Scheduling pipelines is supported only via Python SDK currently (Figure 8-16).

Figure 8-16. *Azure ML workspace pipeline endpoint on the portal*

Let's go ahead and stop the schedule; follow the next cells to stop the schedule (Figure 8-17).

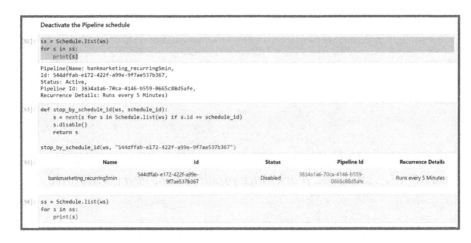

Figure 8-17. *Azure ML workspace pipeline schedule deactivate*

Summary

In this chapter, we explored the basics of *modern* data engineering and the tools that data engineers and data scientists should be familiar with, focusing primarily on Azure Data Factory as the data orchestration tool and Azure Blob Storage (or Data Lake Store) as the storage solution for datasets.

In Chapter 7, we will see how Azure Databricks can easily access Azure Blob and Data Lake Store to load datasets for transformation and analysis purposes. When we look at Azure Synapse, we will also see how Azure Synapse Analytics integrates with Azure Blob and Data Lake Store to load data using Polybase external tables.

Index

A

Apache Spark, 126, 210

Automated Machine Learning (AutoML), 123–125, 146
  definition, 181
  Python SDK, 192–199
  Studio vs. SDK features, 182
  studio web, 182, 183, 185–191
  users, 181

AutoResolveIntegrationRuntime, 94, 114

Azure Blob Storage
  container, 76, 77
  definition, 70
  deployment process, 73–75
  personal computer, difference, 71
  Storage Explorer, 77–80
  types, 72
  UI, 80, 81

Azure container instance (ACI), 174, 176, 177, 199

Azure Databricks
  analytics/business intelligence, 214
  benefits, 213

data engineers
  completeness, 216
  correct format, 216
  data cleanliness, 217, 218
  proper schema, 217
data scientists, 220–222
definition, 10, 213
deploying, 225–227
ecosystem, 215
ELT, 218, 219
exploring
  connecting to clusters, 235–243
  customizing clusters, 232, 234, 235
  data engineering/data science, 227, 228
  Spark compute cluster, 228–231
resources, 11
use cases, 11, 12

Azure Data Factory (ADF)
  accessing on-premises data sources, 111–114
  architecture, 88
  assignment, 97, 99

© Julian Soh and Priyanshi Singh 2020
J. Soh and P. Singh, *Data Science Solutions on Azure*,
https://doi.org/10.1007/978-1-4842-6405-8